CROSSCURRENTS / *Modern Critiques*
Harry T. Moore, *General Editor*

Minor
American Novelists

EDITED BY

Charles Alva Hoyt

WITH A PREFACE BY

Harry T. Moore

SOUTHERN ILLINOIS UNIVERSITY PRESS
Carbondale and Edwardsville

FEFFER & SIMONS, INC.
London and Amsterdam

Contents

v

Preface

As forests shed their foliage by degrees,
So fade expressions which in season please;
And we and ours, alas! are due to fate
And works and words but dwindle to a date.

. . . .

All, all, must perish; but, surviving last,
The love of letters half preserves the past.
True, some decay; yet not a few revive;
Though those shall sink, which now appear to thrive,
As custom arbitrates, whose shifting sway
Our life and language must alike obey.

Byron wrote that in Hints From Horace, which he spoke of in a letter as an "Imitation" of the Roman's Ars Poetica, of which he had so far "translated or varied about 200 lines." The very title of the present book, Minor American Novelists, implies values as well as the "now you're up, now you're down" aspect of literary reputations.

As for the idea of being "minor," Charles Alva Hoyt says, in the Introduction following this Preface, that we shouldn't want to read "major" authors all the time; and certainly we don't. I'm sure a good many of us have read most of the writers discussed in this volume (yes, including John Dickson Carr), and have done so with pleasure.

None of the authors whom Mr. Hoyt's commentators deal with are living except John Dickson Carr. Those among the dead range chronologically from Charles Brockden Brown to Flannery O'Connor. The others in-

clude John William De Forest, Charles Chesnutt, Nathanael West, Edward Lewis Wallant, and James Branch
Cabell—an interesting gallery.

The lives of several of these authors were rather rough;
it has often been observed that the life of a writer in
America is not an easy one. Some of these authors died
fairly young. Edward Lewis Wallant, for example, lived
only from 1926 to 1962. He wrote four novels, as did
Nathanael West (1903–40), killed with his wife (the inspiration of My Sister Eileen) in a California automobile
accident. But, through whatever causes, outward or in-
ward, some of these people seemed doomed not to reach
the age of forty. It is entirely by chance that two essays in
this book, written without collusion, have almost identical endings.

For example, the last sentence of Kenneth Bernard's
discussion of Charles Brockden Brown concludes, "He
died of tuberculosis in 1810 at the age of thirty-nine."
And Paul Levine's essay on Flannery O'Connor ends,
"She died on August 3, 1964, at the age of thirty-nine."
Sed non omnis moriar.

Charles Brockden Brown! I first heard of him in high
school in the 1920s, when one of our texts was William J.
Long's American Literature, first published by Ginn and
Company in 1913. Long was an interesting man; after
being graduated from Harvard and from Andover Theological Seminary, he received his M.A. and Ph.D. from
Heidelberg, also studying at the universities of Paris and
Rome. He became a Congregational clergyman and, I
seem to remember, a friend of Theodore Roosevelt. Long
was a woodsman and wrote various nature books as well
as a history of English Literature and the previously mentioned volume on American literature, one of the first
really comprehensive books on the subject. He even mentioned the then forgotten Melville, in passing, in a sub-
chapter called "Minor Fiction of the First National Period"—there goes that word "minor" again!—but that
was pretty good for 1913. He didn't flinch from Whit-
man, but generously gave him a dozen pages, although

*it is amusing to find him noting that some of the poems
are in "bad taste" and lacking in "moral sense." Still, Long
was quite a guy for his time. It seemed to me only appropriate that he should be mentioned approvingly in one of
the novels I loved in adolescence, before I had been led to
Scott Fitzgerald, immensely superior in the same genre:
Cyril Hume's* Wife of the Centaur, *which John Gilbert
and Eleanor Boardman played in the silent movies. In
this book the poet, newly come to New York from Yale,
meets a pretty girl named Annette who, Jeff is glad to see,
has a copy of one of Long's literary histories.*

Well, that was what might be called a Long paragraph:
but he deserves some little tribute after all these years,
and here it is; I only hope that Long lived to see Hume's
book (Hume, who wound up as a television writer, is also
dead now). But—Charles Brockden Brown, our first
"Gothic" novelist. Long grants him seven pages and
praises his work, though not uncritically. In our book,
Kenneth Bernard shows why Brown is still readable today and mentions several literary histories of the past
(beginning with Brander Matthews' of 1896) which neg-
lected or denigrated Brown (Mr. Bernard missed the
passing swipe at Brown in John Macy's 1913 book, The
Spirit of American Literature), though noting that Arthur Hobson Quinn's Survey in 1936 spoke highly of
him. And I think that Mr. Bernard's own survey gives
us the Charles Brockden Brown we need to know about
today. This is only one fine part of Mr. Hoyt's fine collection of essays.

In this volume Charles William De Forest, discussed
by E. H. Hagemann, follows Brown. He isn't even mentioned in Long's American Literature, perhaps because
his dates (1826–1906) made him seem too recent to a
critic of 1913. Mr. Hagemann, who thinks highly of De
Forest, disarms us at the start by presenting some examples of this novelist's less fortunate attempts at a striking
literary style; but Mr. Hagemann goes on to show us why
De Forest is important and points out that, in five volumes written between 1857 and 1875, he nearly wrote

what might be called "The Great American Novel"—a title De Forest bestowed (no pun intended) on Uncle Tom's Cabin! But, as noted earlier, literary reputations do change. While De Forest (in an anonymous article) was hoisting Uncle Tom, he was lowering the works of Washington Irving, James Fenimore Cooper, and Nathaniel Hawthorne. But let's not hold that against De Forest who, as Mr. Hagemann shows us, wrote some first-rate novels about the Civil War, the postwar South, the depravity of the Grant administration, and other subjects which should interest a good many Americans today. It is interesting to note that De Forest may have been influenced by the then little-known Stendhal.

In speaking of the De Forest books which Mr. Hagemann calls his "Great American Novel," he deals specifically with the two books that close the pentalogy so designated, Honest John Vane and Playing the Mischief. As Mr. Hagemann says, "Never was an era to endure such pitiless, merciless satire. The efforts of Henry Adams and John Hay are ladylike in comparison." Further, in relation to "Honest" John Vane, "De Forest shudders visibly over such troglodytes managing government. And, understandably enough, they escape. But let it be understood that De Forest blames the great American people, the unwashed, for sending an Honest John Vane to the Capital."

De Forest, then, is a man to read: a novelist with a message for today. Would that we had an author capable of portraying fictionally the Washington of our own time! Alas, we have as substitutes such counterfeit novelists as Allen Drury (the criticism here is not personal or ideational, but purely aesthetic); the one serious novelist of our time who attempted such a criticism was John Dos Passos, regrettably caught between the significant creation of the U.S.A. trilogy and the partial regeneration of his earlier talent in Midcentury, and a political epoch that should be understood sympathetically rather than presented satirically. For Washington satire today we have to turn to the hilarious columns of Art Buchwald or the sharply drawn cartoons of Bill Mauldin and Herb

Block, the latter with his special gift for making the cretins in politics look cretinous and the villains, look villainous. In fiction, however, we need another De Forest; but to see how bad things were a century ago, we do have De Forest, and Mr. Hagemann introduces him forcefully.

After the essay on De Forest, we have Robert M. Farnsworth on "Charles Chesnutt and the Color Line." Long doesn't mention Chesnutt (1858–1932), but not because of prejudice, for Long is willing to recognize the black-girl poet of colonial times, Phillis Wheatley, though lamenting her abandonment of her original "barbaric" vision for "drawing-room English" couplets. It was more than a century after Phillis Wheatley that Chesnutt began to write his stories (his first novel didn't appear until 1900), which William Dean Howells welcomed, in a passage Mr. Farnsworth quotes. But Chesnutt, who was a teacher in the South and later a successful businessman in Ohio, didn't produce so much as he might have, for reasons that Mr. Farnsworth indicates are unknown to us. He didn't do so well in writing, financially, as he had hoped to do, though (as Mr. Farnsworth points out) other authors have overcome such discouragements. Howells, who had published Chesnutt's stories in the Atlantic Monthly and had helped him with friendly criticism, apparently didn't care much for his second novel, The Marrow of Tradition (1901), which dealt pinchingly with race relations.

Howells' review of the book showed, Mr. Farnsworth tells us, "the sometimes Sunday School weakness of Howells' position. He does not attack the literary weakness of the novel, where he could perhaps have been most helpful, but he suggests the grudging reluctance of the white audience to accept emotionally what it cannot in all conscience deny"—a bitterness. The condition has changed at least slightly over the years. Maybe all whites don't accept the powerful novels written by blacks today —but surely the Howellses of our time do.

At this point—and I'm running out of space—I'm going to skip the next writer discussed in Mr. Hoyt's book,

James Branch Cabell, and save him for the last, largely because he is in a special way controversial. I don't think there's much I can say about John Dickson Carr, whom I've earlier admitted that I've enjoyed reading—the Gideon Fell mysteries, though not the "historical" reconstructions. The whodunit type of writing is a special kind of subject matter, and though I began reading the Sherlock Holmes stories when I was a kid and have followed those up with the works of Dorothy L. Sayers and "Michael Innes" and on to Ian Fleming and John Le Carré, I wouldn't attempt any comments on the genre except to say it is relaxing; and I find the comments of Roger Herzel, who is both personal and inquiring about the matter, suitably entertaining. Carr remains "minor" enough, and no one will try to promote him; and most of his writing is fun to read. As I said, I like Dr. Fell, whom Mr. Herzel properly designates as "genial"; and Fell is amusingly brilliant, too, as Mr. Herzel demonstrates.

Bruce Olsen's essay on Nathanael West points out that West was, although nominally the author of four novels, actually the author of one and a half: Miss Lonelyhearts and the "unfulfilled novel about Hollywood, The Day of the Locust." That's a fair enough judgment, though most of us can enjoy most of West, as Edmund Wilson, James F. Light, and even Mr. Olsen himself show us. True, Mr. Olsen finds "labored wit" in A Cool Million, as well as many other flaws, and he very plausibly shows us why it isn't up to Miss Lonelyhearts; yet he finds it "praiseworthy by most extrinsic standards," though in other ways "a failure." Even the first novel, The Dream Life of Balso Snell, partly written while West was still an undergraduate at Brown University, has, for Mr. Olsen, "promise" even in its "immaturity." He carefully qualifies all his statements—and there is no room here to mention his qualifications, so that one can only say they are shrewd and convincing. At the last he finds West the author of one book which achieved "objectivity" (Miss Lonelyhearts) and of one which almost achieved it another time (The Day of the Locust). Mr. Olsen doesn't sentimentalize over the potential of an author who was

killed at a comparatively young age, but one can certainly
be sad about it. West of course remains another "minor"
novelist who won't be promoted, but what an artistic
pleasure it is to reread the cynically sad Miss Lonelyhearts; and the hell with today's sobsisters.

How many of these people died young—we now come
to Flannery O'Connor, so ably discussed by Paul Levine.
He begins by mentioning several authors in relation to
her, first Saul Bellow, in passing, and then Sherwood
Anderson who, like Miss O'Connor, wrote of "grotesques." And then Mr. Levine introduces a long section
on Nathanael West which fits in neatly. Later, Mr.
Levine refers to Norman Mailer and other authors, but
only to extend the scope of his background. He doesn't
mention the wasting disease of Flannery O'Connor's last
years, but he does end with that sudden sentence, previously quoted, about her early death. In his explication
of her work, however, he brings it to life, and he makes
plain why her rural Southern stories are so forceful. His
exploration of her use of language (the word "style" is
too suggestive of artifice) is particularly valuable.

Charles Alva Hoyt, the resourceful editor of this
book—an expert on Victorian literature and chairman
of an English department, he is also a professional jazz
pianist—is no stranger to the Crosscurrents series, since
his essays have appeared here in collections edited by
others, and he has himself edited books for it. Early in
his present essay, Mr. Hoyt says that Edward Lewis
Wallant "can be considered 'minor' only in terms of
what he might have done had he lived beyond the age of
thirty-six." Like Nathanael West, Wallant wrote four
novels, the best known of which is The Pawnbroker,
which after the author's death was filmed in Hollywood.
Wallant, who died of aneurism, didn't live to see his
last two novels in print.

Mr. Hoyt gives us valuable insights into Wallant's
fiction, finding as its center "the sudden hunger to know
what lies in the hearts of others" (a quotation from
Wallant), "or rather, as the theme characteristically appears in a framework of exhortation, the absolute obliga-

tion of all men to acknowledge this hunger and to satisfy it by communion with their fellows"—an essentially Romantic battle cry which Mr. Hoyt has heard in such recent works as Franny and Zooey (J. D. Salinger), A New Life (Bernard Malamud), Henderson the Rain King (Saul Bellow), and One Flew over the Cuckoo's Nest (Ken Kesey). And even D. H. Lawrence is invoked. Beyond such generalities and points of relativity, however, Mr. Hoyt provides us with some examinations of Wallant's writings which are both thorough and illuminating.

The essay on Wallant ends this book impressively, but earlier I said that I would deal with the one on James Branch Cabell last. One of my reasons is that I dislike Cabell, even as a "minor" writer—yet I like the man who wrote the essay on him. Incidentally, I always disliked Cabell, even when I first read him in the 1920s.

In a previous book Mr. Hoyt edited for the Crosscurrents series, I mentioned that one of its contributors, Fred B. Millett was one of my teachers at the University of Chicago. He is now Professor Emeritus of Wesleyan University, and Mr. Hoyt in his Introduction (I never heard Fred Millett called "Frederick" before) pays appropriate tribute to his scholarly and administrative abilities, mentioning Mr. Millett's particular achievements.

It is just forty years since I was first a student of his, in a course in Contemporary British Literature, summer quarter 1930, which assembled about two hundred; and I was a student of his in subsequent classes. In my career as a university student I had several great teachers (including Philip Schuyler Allen, who must always go first, Thornton Wilder, Moody Prior, Angelo Bertocci, Gerald Warner Brace, and Edward Wagenknecht); and Fred B. Millett stands among them. Before he retired, I used to talk with him at the annual meetings of the Modern Language Association, and now we exchange greetings across distances; and I continue to find his books extremely valuable.

My disagreement with his Cabell essay will of course

only amuse him, and it is in any event a well-meant, friendly disagreement. He has power on his side, Edmund Wilson, say—but modern America's most brilliant master of synopsis and explication can sometimes be terribly wrong in his literary judgments.

Mr. Millett cites other critics and, as a kind of indirect proof of Cabell's lasting qualities, mentions that a number of books on him by younger men have appeared recently (Mr. Millett lists them in his notes); I can only find this appalling.

Besides giving his own opinions of Cabell, generally favorable, Mr. Millett quotes several critics (besides Wilson) on the subject of this author. Two he treats rather harshly: Peter Monro Jack and Oscar Cargill. The late Peter Monro Jack used to review regularly for the New York Times Book Review; his disparagement of Cabell appeared in a volume edited by Malcolm Cowley, After the Genteel Tradition, whose revised edition this Press is proud to publish in its Crosscurrents series. I think that Peter Jack made out an excellent and enduring case against Cabell. The criticism by Oscar Cargill that Mr. Millett refers to is from Intellectual America: Ideas on the March, which is characterized as being "so extravagant that it belongs with the literature of vituperation and not with criticism." Well, really, Mr. Millett! It's hard to find one old friend berating another (I had the pleasure of teaching in Mr. Cargill's English department when he was chairman at the Washington Square College of New York University, where I taught there in the evenings of one summer while teaching at Columbia in the mornings). In the Crosscurrents series we have happily published a book by Oscar Cargill, Toward a Pluralistic Criticism, in which he makes some incidental but biting references to Cabell.

Well, Cabell is still a phony to me, and I don't care what Wilson, or V. L. Parrington, or Carl Van Doren says. Incidentally, Mr. Millett doesn't mention the antagonism to Cabell expressed in Granville Hicks's The Great Tradition, first published in 1933. Granville Hicks, it seems to me, became a very fine critic years later; I think that his book, called The Great Tradition (Ah, Leavis!) is, despite some remarkable insights, for the most part ill-digested Marxism. Malcolm Cowley's review of the first edition of the book in the New Republic of November 8, 1933 (reprinted in the Southern Illinois Press's collection of Cowley's essays, edited by Henry Dan Piper, Think Back on Us . . .), was in the form of a letter to Mr. Hicks which praised his book but found some faults in it: "Thus, granting the truth of everything you say about James Branch Cabell's books, I can see no justification of your ascribing a 'fundamental venality' to their author; phrases like this belong elsewhere than in a history of literature." I hazily remember that, sometime later, still qualifying his praise, Malcolm Cowley spoke well again of Granville Hicks's words on Cabell, particularly the paragraph beginning, "This Virginia gentleman and geneologist . . ." It contains the "fundamental venality" phrase, however, which Mr. Hicks didn't change in the later editions. I agree with Malcolm Cowley's objection, as well as with his approval of much that the book said about Cabell, who always was, to me, an author who seemed, to use our colloquial phrase once again, a phony.

Differences of opinion—literary quarrels—at least they can be conducted at the level of gentlemen's disagreement. There is no need for us to follow the pungent Dr. Johnson of the eighteenth century, who dismissed Jonathan Swift so sneeringly: "The dog never hazards a metaphor." In our own time, criticism was comparatively genteel until recently, when one mad dog among critics infected a whole kennel, somewhat in "the great tradition." Oh well, let that go. I don't care for Cabell, but don't dislike people who speak well of him, and that's that.

As for the present book—by way of conclusion—it is informative and often profoundly interesting.

HARRY T. MOORE

Southern Illinois University
April 23, 1970

Introduction

"Minor figure!" cries a character from Molière (*Les Femme Savantes*, translated and adapted by one of our contributors, Mr. Roger Herzel) – "Minor figure! Sir, you have insulted me and I must challenge you to a duel!" And indeed, what author, commencing his career, would settle for such a nomination? Few authors at the close of their careers have been willing to accept it; a self-evaluation so dispassionate as Max Beerbohm's is rare among writers, or among men in general. Max may be pointed at as the minor figure par excellence: he selected a little niche, as he himself has told us, and filled it decoratively. And he is useful in reminding us that the minor figure may be the most pleasant of companions. Who would wish to spend all his time with George Eliot, Thomas Hardy, William Wordsworth? Who, if condemned to do so, would not sneak away for frequent and prolonged visits with Conan Doyle, John Aubrey, or Saki?

The authors discussed in this book are generally considered, at present, to be minor ones. The reasons for this judgment are various: in some cases, like that of E. L. Wallant, premature death prevented the man from building up a large body of work (although what he has left us may raise him in the estimation of the next age). In others, as in that of John Dickson Carr, the author has applied himself almost exclusively, or most successfully, to a certain rather restricted genre, one which automatically confers minor status. Here I hope I may be allowed to refer to the Introduction which I wrote for the companion volume to this book, *Minor British Novelists* (Southern Illinois University Press, 1967). There I remarked that minor status seems often to be the result not of a writer's gifts, but of his conception and ambition. The major novelists have their crotchets, as do the minor ones, but, as I put it in my earlier essay, the major figure conceives of his preoccupation in terms of the whole world, while the minor can see the world only in terms of his preoccupation.

Having examined that pronouncement once again, and come once again to the belief that in spite of its resonance, it actually says something, I permit myself one more observation before introducing the contributors to this volume. A critic of *Minor British Novelists* was disappointed because the essays which appeared in it did not adhere to one theme, or follow one turn of thought. What disappointed him, delighted me; in fact I had conceived of the volume with the ideal before me of a rich *olla podrida* of varying opinions and approaches. Once again I have succeeded in pleasing myself and, I'm afraid, angering this and perhaps other critics. I can only say that our subjects here—some of the most vigorous, highly individual personalities in our literature—resist the editorial embalmer with a most commendable stoutness.

And now the contributors, in the order in which they appear. The first is Kenneth Bernard, Associate Professor of English at Long Island University. A playwright and often-published poet as well as a scholar, Professor Bernard has produced numerous articles on American literature, in journals as diverse as *College English* and *Playboy*. E. R. Hagemann, next in line, is known as a prolific writer on American literature, particularly that of the late nineteenth century. After having taught at UCLA and served some time in business, he came to the University of Louisville in 1964, where he is now Professor and chairman of the department.

Robert Farnsworth, Professor of English at the University of Missouri, Kansas City, is a specialist on the literature of the American Negro. In connection with his work in this field he has published among other things considerable criticism of the work of Charles Chesnutt, the author with whom he has chosen to deal in this volume. Our next man is Frederick B. Millett, Professor Emeritus at Wesleyan, Head of Honors College there and a former national president of AAUP—that rarest of combinations, the good administrator and true scholar. His works are in use everywhere today; perhaps we need mention only his enormously influential *Contemporary American Authors.*

Passing from our senior contributor to our junior, we come to Mr. Roger Herzel, who is located at Cedar Crest College, where he teaches Creative Writing and Dramatic Literature. Mr. Herzel is a recent graduate of Haverford and a candidate for the Ph.D. degree at Johns Hopkins; besides mystery fiction he is interested in French, having translated plays by Marivaux and Molière, as noted above. Bruce Olsen, the departmental chairman at Briarcliffe, is also a man of parts, a novelist and philosopher as well as a critic who has conducted a number of forays into the Theory of Style. Nathanael West is a long-time favorite of his.

From the University of Toronto, Paul Levine, sometime of Wesleyan, Harvard, and Rochester. Mr. Levine holds the rank of Associate Professor at Toronto; his numerous articles and studies are principally on the subject of contemporary literature. His current book, at this writing, is appropriately titled *The Intemperate Zone: The Climate of Contemporary Literature.* Finally, the editor, Charles Alva Hoyt, myself: Professor and Chairman of English at Bennett College. Trained at Wesleyan and Columbia as a nineteenth-century specialist, he has undertaken more and more to study contemporary literature; this is his fifth appearance in Southern Illinois University Press's *Crosscurrents* series. He has also published his way through a wide range of periodicals including *Encyclopedia Americana,* the New

York *Times, Saturday Review, Commonweal,* and *Gourmet. Bon appétit* to the reader of this book.

CHARLES   ALVA   HOYT

Millbrook, New York
June 1969

Charles Brockden Brown

KENNETH BERNARD

Like any great artist of story, like Shakespeare or Balzac or Dickens or Dostoevski, James crowds probability rather closer than we nowadays like. It is not that he gives us unlikely events but that he sometimes thickens the number of interesting events beyond our ordinary expectation. If this, in James or in any storyteller, leads to a straining of our sense of verisimilitude, there is always the defense to be made that the special job of literature is, as Marianne Moore puts it, the creation of "Imaginary gardens with real toads in them." The reader who detects that the garden is imaginary should not be led astray by his discovery to a wrong view of the reality of the toads. In settling questions of reality and truth in fiction, it must be remembered that, although the novel in certain of its forms resembles the accumulative and classificatory sciences, which are the sciences most people are at home with, in certain other of its forms the novel approximates the sciences of experiment. And an experiment is very like an imaginary garden which is laid out for the express purpose of supporting a real toad of fact. The apparatus of the researcher's bench is not nature itself but an artificial and extravagant contrivance, much like a novelist's plot, which is devised to force or foster a fact into being.
— Lionel Trilling, *The Liberal Imagination*

The key to any understanding of Charles Brockden Brown (1771–1810) is an awareness of the tension between utopianism and a puritan pessimism that infused his life and his work. Brown's novels seem often to reflect a mind excited with hope for man and society, a hope based on the infinite possibilities of human thought. Yet this hope always founders on those dim borders where man ceases to be a rational creature, beyond which loom potentialities as dark as the others are bright. For all Brown's faith in man's ability to improve himself through the rational faculties, the darkness beckons and he follows in spite of himself. It is a truth he cannot fully understand, but which he cannot avoid. Harry Levin has aptly written that Brown "was completely committed to the postulates of the Enlightenment; and light itself is an almost compulsive source of his imagery." "Ironically but not illogically," he adds, "one of the consequences of light is an intensification of shadow." [1] It is out of this dichotomy that Brown creates his elaborate, elusive plots, which in turn nourish his real, albeit monstrous, toads.

The rationalism and social protest of the eighteenth century, particularly that of such writers as Mary Wollstonecraft and William Godwin, are obvious formative influences on his mind. As a youth, Brown, being sickly and hence sedentary, indulged a capacity for broad learning which was to be reflected throughout his short life. [2] His literary pursuits, too, were on a large scale, as indicated by his projected catalog of all knowledge and teenage plans for epics on the discovery of America, Pizarro's conquest of Peru, and Cortez's expedition to Mexico. Add to these his classical studies at Robert Proud's Quaker School and the fact that Philadelphia was a city buoyant with talk of revolution and reform, made even more exciting by the presence of refugees and travelers from France and England, and it is not difficult to see the ferment of Brown's young mind and to understand how his faith in the powers of reason to perfect man's earthly condition developed.

However, there was another side to Brown. The solitary walks which Proud had encouraged as an aid to health gave the boy a chance to brood. Raised a Quaker, he was no stranger to the inner life, which in his case tended toward the somber. As an adult he urged his friends to be frank, revealing all in their letters; but in return he was meager, saying that his "own heart shall be the depository of its own gloomy sensations." [3] Nor could it be said that the pervasive puritanism of an earlier period was dissipated, even in the federal capital. Throughout Brown's work, doubts about the nature of man and his potentialities, surprising revelations of his weakness and finitude, keep breaking through the rational, optimistic framework. A further stimulus to Brown's interest in the finite and the nonrational was his close friendship with Elihu Hubbard Smith. Smith was not only a student of Benjamin Rush, a pioneer researcher into mental aberration, but he conducted his own investigations into abnormal psychology and contributed to the *Medical Repository*, a magazine Brown read. Finally there was Brown's own wide reading in Gothic fiction. To be sure, he inclined to Mrs. Radcliffe's brand of rational explanation of strange phenomena; his use of ventriloquism and sleepwalking are, on the surface, attempts to ground strange actions in startling but verifiable data, that is, reason. Yet a careful reading of books like *Wieland* and *Edgar Huntly* reveals mystery rather than explanation, darkness rather than light. He was far more influenced by Godwin's *Caleb Williams* than by *Political Justice*; and he liked *Caleb Williams* not for the lesson Godwin thought it was, but for its psychological probing into the nonrational in human behavior.

Brown began his adult life studying law in the office of a prominent lawyer in Philadelphia. It was considered a most suitable profession, and when he left it in 1793 to pursue a literary career, he caused his family much grief. In an early work, he reflects his attitude toward the "trade" by confessing, "I fear I shall never untie legal knots or dissensolve from this maze by already bewildered understanding." [4] In view of his intellectual capacities and his affinities for the powers of reason, Brown's abandonment of the law is surprising—unless one bears in mind that other influences were at work on him, influences that account for his "already bewildered un-

derstanding." Thereafter, Brown shuttled between Philadelphia and New York, writing his early works, *Alcuin,
A Dialogue on the Rights of Women* and *Sky-Walk*.
The former particularly reveals what one early critic
called his "indefinite dreams of perfectibility." [5] Of *Alcuin* he wrote, "It exhibits the crude and fanciful specu-
lations of a theorist, who, in his dreams of optimism,
charges exclusively on human institutions the imperfec-
tions necessarily incident to human nature." [6] Brown was
not, however, to continue to fulfill this image. In 1798
he moved to New York and began the scrambled activity
that in three years produced his six novels, the first four
of which, *Wieland, Ormond, Arthur Mervyn,* and *Edgar
Huntly,* radically challenge the image of the dreamy
utopian that his early works suggest to some.

This contradiction in Brown can best be seen in his
major villains. They are of two kinds, villains of light
and villains of dark. The first are men of great intellect,
however imperfectly portrayed, heirs of the Enlightenment, men whose assaults on society are the result of
their powers of rational thought. Brown's sources for
such men were the secret societies like the Illuminati
and Gothic heroes like Radcliffe's Schedoni. Men like
Ormond, Ludloe, Carwin, and Welbeck perpetrate evil
on principle. Their goals, when they are known, are
usually nothing less than the perfect society, and beyond
the understanding and ability of the ordinary man.
Hence they operate on a level of morality that seems
immorality, finally verging on the demonic. But to them
their methods are merely a higher means to a higher
end.

These high-minded villains, kin to so many of Hawthorne's cold practitioners on human beings, represent
the impact of eighteenth-century rationalism on Brown,
as well as his own Faustian appetite carried to extremes.
That they clearly *are* evil is testimony to the fact that
Brown, almost in spite of himself, found the powers of
rational thought insufficient to explain or solve the problems of man and society, just as for Hawthorne the

unpardonable sin was an intellectual one. Such men must be struck down for their intellectual arrogance and moral blindness. Ormond, in the book titled after him, destroys Constantia Dudley's father as he would a fly because he opposes her alliance with him. To Ormond this is just, because his union with Constantia is a greater good than Dudley's life. Ormond is a man of superior, even superb, intellect, but he cannot see the evil which to Brown is so obvious. Brown arranges his death with suitable irony. Ormond's one lapse from his unprincipled rationalism is his genuine passion for Constantia. It is this which causes his death, for Constantia, against all *reason*, refuses to love him on his terms. In a rage, acting against all his principles, he attempts to rape her, and she kills him. But Ormond's lapse also rescues him from complete abstraction by humanizing him. There is, in the end, an aura of tragedy about his death.

Of Brown's villains of light, only Ormond is complete. Ludloe, in "Carwin the Biloquist," is fragmentary. And Carwin and Welbeck in *Wieland* and *Arthur Mervyn* are ambiguous because they partake of Brown's other major villains, the villains of dark. There are only two such villains in Brown, Wieland, from the book named after him, and Clithero in *Edgar Huntly*. These are creatures who spring from the nonrational corners of the mind. Their sustenance comes from darkness and mystery. Clithero, deep in the jagged bowels of the earth, high atop an isolated pinnacle, surrounded by blackness and danger, a veritable prince of chaos, is the perfect image. The passions of these villains, rivaling the elements in their primordial strength, bear no comparison with the refined and rational enthusiasms of a Ludloe or an Ormond. Brown was not quite sure what to make of them. Hence his clumsy use of the strange phenomena of his day like ventriloquism and sleepwalking, which explain, but do not explain enough. For Brown they are a feeble attempt to objectify his shapeless yet penetrating insights into human character. The failure of villains like Carwin and Welbeck is that they begin as villains of light, become crossed with villains of dark, and "in the end apparently accept the validity of ordinary moral values, and seem to know remorse." [7] Brown retreats to convention. Warren Barton Blake, writing of the recognition accorded Washington Irving in England, says, "The same might be true of Brown had he acted on the principle that art is properly either representative or symbolical." [8] The remark illuminates Brown's confusion of villain. Brown's villains of light are clearly intended as "representative," that is, realistic; they reveal Brown's intellectual synthesis of man and society. His heroes of dark, in contrast, are "symbolical"; they objectify Brown's inchoate intuitions. It is the failure of the former and the success of the latter—in the narratives themselves, in Brown's conception of them, and in the power of their presentation—that indicates the true direction of Brown's mind. It is interesting to note here that when Brown writes of his heroes of light, notably in *Ormond* and *Arthur Mervyn*, his settings are "representative," he strives for realistic depiction, as for example in his famous plague scenes; but when he writes of his other heroes, as in *Wieland* and *Edgar Huntly*, his settings are remarkably "symbolical," as in the cave scenes of *Huntly*, an insufficiently noted characteristic that makes him an important forerunner of Cooper, Hawthorne, Poe, and later writers.[9]

A short sketch in the *Weekly Register* in 1798 reveals Brown's ambivalence in another way. An old ugly man named Linehoff calls for his pigs so oddly that the children run after him, imitating "Pig! pig! pig!" Furious but unable to stop them, humiliated beyond endurance, Linehoff moves to another town, where, years later one of the boys, now grown, sees him and cannot refrain from shouting "Pig! pig! pig!" Linehoff turns as if stung by a rattlesnake, leaves, then returns and nearly kills the man, whereupon he is sent to prison, leaving a sick wife. His neighbors describe him as a quiet, hardworking man. Brown cites the story as a demonstration of the folly of ridicule. It is typical of Brown to use material whose intrinsic worth is deeply psychological, material that deals with the perverse, tortuous, mystifying nature of man, and to superimpose upon it a rationale that has little or no relationship with the real sources of vitality in that material. He was instinctively drawn to such material, but his intellectual inheritance contaminated his use of it.

Thus, on the surface Brown's novels easily seem tracts for the rational philosophies of his day. *Wieland,* for example, is a protest against the excesses to which religious passion, or any passion, may lead; *Arthur Mervyn* demonstrates that it is encumbent on all enlightened people to feel benevolence toward all mankind. The novels are filled with progressive *mots* like this Godwinian one by Clara Wieland: "But setting these considerations aside, was it laudable to grasp at wealth and power even when they were within our reach? Were not these the two great sources of depravity?" But in fact Brown had other, less obvious preoccupations, which place him more firmly in the tradition of American literature and make it possible to see him as a transition figure between the Enlightenment and the romantic period. For example, in *Arthur Mervyn* and in *Edgar Huntly* he creates a complex alter ego relationship. Mervyn's innocence is compromised by the Satanic Welbeck. Through Welbeck, Mervyn becomes involved in evil. Their lives entwine; each one has an inexplicable fascination for the other. But Mervyn does not, finally, repudiate Welbeck's influence. He accepts it and even praises it because it has been the means of his greater understanding of the world. And in *Edgar Huntly,* throughout most of the book Clithero functions as the dark, subconscious side of Huntly's personality; the book is an elaborate narration of Huntly's struggle to remain in possession of his mind.[10] Brown's psychological insight in this work and elsewhere can only be called prodigious. One enthusiastic commentator has written, no doubt a little too jauntily: "In the matter of morbid analysis,

Poe, in comparison with Brown, was superficial, Hawthorne was cheerful, and the modern school of French writers are feeble." [11] Yet he was not too far wrong. And an anonymous commentator in 1918, again echoing the small but steady response to Brown for a century, wrote of him, "He is said to have worked too violently in composition to produce calm and deliberate narrative. Nevertheless he was more akin to these modern psychologists like Dostoevsky than any of the later realists are." [12] However, many histories of American literature barely mentioned Brown,[13] and some denigrated him considerably: "He was a romancer of the old kind . . . he has no art; he is awkward, long-winded, and melodramatic, interested almost wholly in adventure, and save for the accident of coming first and being a philadelphian would be without note." [14]

Although there was some enthusiastic response to Brown's four novels, his friends, family, and public found them morbid. Too few were aware that his efforts had been pioneering, that, as one recent critic wrote, "Under his touch the abnormal took on dignity." [15] As if to mark off the end of his creative period, Brown returned to Philadelphia in 1801 and entered into business partnership with his two brothers. He published two more novels, *Clara Howard* and *Jane Talbot*, both departures from his earlier work but not without interest. Colden, the male protagonist of *Jane Talbot*, is a dim reflection of Brown's villains of light. He even illustrates, at one point, the debilitating effects on character of too much reason. However, primarily the books return to one of Brown's earliest interests, the role of women in society. Both novels are cast to the theme of love versus duty. *Jane Talbot* in particular is far better than most critics have claimed, Brown there portraying a woman of intellect, wit, and charm who was not to be duplicated in American literature until James.

Brown married in 1804. He had four children and seems to have enjoyed family life very much. He remained in a small way in business for several years, busied himself with editorial duties, composed political tracts. He wrote no more fiction. His career as a novelist had been short and feverish. He died of tuberculosis in 1810 at the age of thirty-nine.

John William De Forest's "Great American Novel"

E. R. HAGEMANN

For a moment, let us consider this passage from *Seacliff* (1859), John William De Forest's mystery novel, as Louis Fitz Hugh rhapsodizes his beloved Mary Westervelt:

I had met a beautiful lady in alien lands;—I had lost her among awful mountain gleams and thick vapors;—I had tracked her over multitudinous billows, and found her once more;—I had seen her flying in extremest peril, with death following hard after. (p. 81)

Or, this passage, as the same Fitz Hugh comments on Louis Somerville's voice:

Nothing could be more demulcent and basalmic; it made me think of anodynes and cherry pectorals; it was enough to cure a cold to hear him talk. (pp. 61–62)

Or, a third passage, this one from *The Wetherel Affair* (1873), as the lovers, Edward Wetherel and Nestoria Bernard, are united:

Without a word he advanced softly to her, knelt on one knee at her foot, took both her hands in his and kissed them passionately.

"Oh, no, no, no! I am not worthy," broke out Nestoria, the tears rolling down her cheeks. "You must not show me any kindness. . . . I am unworthy of your trust. I have wronged you dreadfully and unpardonably." (p. 218)

Not a very impressive introduction to John William De Forest, so often hailed and saluted as an important literary realist in American fiction. But the point of this is to get into the consideration in hand evidence that he was capable of some lamentably bad writing. There is no reason to ignore this. After all, any good writer is capable of wretched passages. Twain, for example. Or Scott Fitzgerald.

But I am not concerned with these two novels, or with *Justine's Lovers* (1878) or *Irene the Missionary* (1879). They can be dismissed as irrelevant to my purpose: a discussion, analysis, and evaluation of what amounts to a "Great American Novel" written by De Forest during the period 1857–75. The quotation marks are used for a double purpose: the product is not one novel but, in fact, five, and the product is that all-time *ignis fatuus* in American letters never to be captured, perhaps, although De Forest came pretty close in his day.

"The Great American Novel" is also the title of a significant article De Forest published (anonymously) in the *Nation* in 1868, about seven months after the appearance of *Miss Ravenel's Conversion*. Opening his case, De Forest speaks of "a friend of ours" who cherishes the "craze" that he will, some day, write a great American novel. But will he do it? De Forest asks. Very doubtful, indeed; the obstacles are immense. But there have been some attempts at "painting the American soul" within its framework. De Forest then considers, and rejects, Washington Irving ("too cautious to make the trial"), Fenimore Cooper (he "shirked" the task), Nathaniel Hawthorne (too parochial). No. These men and their novels will not do. The one novel that most closely approaches "The Great American Novel" is *Uncle Tom's Cabin*, despite its faulty plot; for it has "a national breadth" to it and is "a picture of American life," not filled in finally but still "a portrait."

De Forest considers other writers: James Kirke Paulding, Charles Brockden Brown, John Pendleton Kennedy, W. Gilmore Simms, Oliver Wendell Holmes (of all people), and Rebecca Harding Davis. But they, too, will not do.

He asks the question: "Is there . . . a single tale which paints American life so broadly, truly, and sympathetically that every American of feeling and culture is forced to acknowledge the picture as a likeness of something which he knows?" Excepting *Uncle Tom's Cabin*, the answer is "No." Why? A lack of an international copyright is one reason. Another and more important reason is that the United States changes too rapidly to be "fixed" to a single canvas; the nation is composed of too many "component parts" to be collected together in one novel.

I have said that this article had appeared some seven months after *Miss Ravenel's Conversion*, sufficient time then for the American reading public to have recognized that it was *the* American novel; however, the public did not so recognize and it did not sell. Thus there is every chance that in speaking of a "friend," De Forest was either implying himself or actually speaking of himself. It rankled him, doubtless, to see his novel go begging, for he had managed to accomplish what Fitz Hugh had spoken of in *Seacliff*: to gather all his "intellectual effort and emotional nature in one effort." Nevertheless De Forest realized that even though he had done this, the novel was not precisely The Great American Novel for the very reasons he listed in the *Nation*.

So it was then, to my way of thinking, that De Forest set himself his future task: making the sum total of his novel-output The Great American Novel; that is, each novel henceforth would add another "part" to the whole, and the whole would be a social, economic, political, and, above all, realistic picture of the United States from Colonial times to the present dark days of the Grant administration. He was not altogether successful; not *every* novel contributed significantly and esthetically to this scheme; some must be cast out by any level-headed critic. He also had already on hand two novels, *Witching Times* and *Miss Ravenel's Conversion*, which he could utilize. Eventually eight of his novels served: *Witching Times* (the Salem witch trials), *A Lover's*

Revolt (the Revolution), *Kate Beaumont* (antebellum South), *Miss Ravenel's Conversion* (the Civil War), *Honest John Vane* and *Playing the Mischief* (Grant administration politics), *The Bloody Chasm* (Reconstruction), and *Overland* (the American West).

By dismissing three of these, *A Lover's Revolt*, *The Bloody Chasm*, and *Overland* as too shallow and weak for serious consideration, we still have five remaining, and they form what can be called (to devise a word) a pentalogy—and "The Great American Novel." These are De Forest's best novels and one of them, *Miss Ravenel*, his very best.

As bad as *The Wetherel Affair* is as a novel it is nevertheless interesting as a presentation of De Forest's politics in the broadest sense. He emerges here as a good conservative, Tory-like democrat who is loyal to the idea of an elite group in control of affairs of government and society. He is horrified by a nation which would suffer itself "to be ruled politically by its non-taxpayers" and which degrades its judiciary by making it look toward meetings for power and honor. He has a paternalistic attitude toward the laboring classes; he would, through lecture courses, spell out for them the proper economic and social courses for their lives.

In an obscure article, "The High-Toned Gentlemen," in the *Nation*, March 12, 1868, he had advised his countrymen (let us say, Northerners) to save from the ruins of the Confederacy "every idea or sentiment which may add value to our own social edifice." Specifically, he had in mind the Southern gentleman who represented to him the moral man in public life. De Forest was fearful of his "probable successor, the 'gentleman of democracy,'" i.e., the professional politician who had none of the Southerner's (or well-bred New Englander's) probity as an office-holder. Is this person in "a sufficiently forward state," he asks, to replace the "chivalrous Southron" without leaving us in an "interregnum of vulgarity"? Politics, De Forest asserts solemnly, deserves "the care of the best and the wisest." Although in *Kate*

Beaumont he was to score the "Southron" for certain sins of commission and omission, here he asks assimilation by the entire nation, North and South, of the "better peculiarities" of these men whom he found so difficult to dislike, men (his fictional characters) like Judge McAlister, Peyton Beaumont, and Colonel John Kershaw who, despite personal defects and enslaved by the code *duello*, are faultless men in public affairs. If such worthy men held public office, then the attacks by the "gentlemen of democracy" could be headed. This was De Forest's fond hope.

Any such hope failed of realization, and the assault succeeded in the disarray of General Grant's two administrations, as a morally-tattered band of politicians, manipulators, lobbyists, and grafters poured through the breach and into the miasma of Washington. The "Land-Sharks," an important concept in De Forest's work, were here to stay.

"Land-Shark" was first used in *Seacliff*—it would seem that De Forest used his lesser novels and obscure articles to try his ideas and then refine them in his better things as he needed them. Henry Van Leer brings the conversation around to his favorite sport, shark-fishing. Jenny Westervelt maliciously inquires if there are such things as "Land-Sharks." Robert Van Leer does not understand.

"By Land-Sharks," said [Fitz Hugh] . . . "I suppose Miss Genevieve means mermen; fellows of an amphibious, doubtful, brutal nature, who creep unsuspected into human society and fill it with troubles."

"Exactly," replied Genevieve; "all such outlandish creatures as gamblers, rakes, roués, and hateful people generally."

"That is a clever fancy," observed Somerville,—"that wicked people are not of the human race, but steal in among us from some outcast species, commit their evil deeds, and then, perhaps, return for safety to their own place." (p. 25)

Somerville has described himself and all "Land-Sharks" perfectly. De Forest attached much importance to them, for they appear in one shape or another, greater or lesser, in all but one of his novels, *Irene the Missionary*, together with the assaults on the ramparts of his ideal republic in his "Great American Novel": *Witching Times*, in which the witch-hunts were the first assault on the ideal; *Kate Beaumont*, in which slavery and its attendant evils was the second assault; *Miss Ravenel's Conversion*, in which the Civil War was the third assault; and *Honest John Vane* and *Playing the Mischief*, in which politics was the fourth assault. All assaults seem to fail in this schematization, except politics, always viewed through a glass darkly by De Forest. Naturally enough, as he considers each assault, he also has much to say about his country.

Since *Witching Times* was serialized only in *Putnam's Monthly Magazine*, December 1856 through September 1857, and did not receive book publication until very recently, its importance in the development of the historical novel in America has been pretty much overlooked. Indeed it was not until 1930 that any recognition at all was given it when G. Harrison Orians, writing in *American Literature*, called it "by far the fullest treatment of Salem witchcraft." It was "the only fictional treatment which covers the entire period of the Salem distresses, and provides a comprehensive and psychological account of actors, scenes, and motives in that mad delusion." The reader should remember that many of the "actors" are accurately rendered historical personages.

Relentlessly, De Forest depicts the progress of the land sharks in Salem, Elders Samuel Parris and Nicholas Noyes, Samuel Sewall, and Cotton Mather, and their juggernaut of witchery as it gains slowly more and more ground and the churches fill as never before. Against the sharks and their packs of fanatic believers stand the intellectual (and fictional) Henry More, Mark Stanton, and Giles Cory. These three men have seceded from the evil of Salem and declared themselves loyal to the idea of good in society; or, to state the situation another way, the populace of the wretched Salem, led by the elders and justices, have seceded from the good. However stated, this is another important facet of De Forest's thinking, this conception of secession. It is realized more fully in *Miss Ravenel's Conversion* but the early development of secession and loyalty in American society is in *Witching Times*.

His loyalty and opposition to the juggernaut bring about More's trial on September 17, 1692, in First Church. To assure victory, the land sharks bring yet another such into their company, the prosecuting attorney, Thomas Newton. More does not stand a chance, and, his brilliant defense of no account, he is found guilty. But this secessionist has his final say in court. He connects Elder Parris and Titus Oates, the latter "the great exemplar and forerunner" of Parris.

Let it be noted, that this is an age of such men; an age of false accusers and fabricated conspiracies. Titus Oates was the founder of a new style of wickedness, which, since his day, has become our peculiar national sin, and will, some day, work out its peculiar national judgment. (Chap. 9, p. 412)

More is executed on the gibbet.

Then, when the fantasy has all but disappeared, when their damage has been done, the land sharks, Mather, Parrish, Noyes, prolixly reflect and sanctimoniously rationalize their roles in the affair. Mather, for one, rather expansively points out that other instances of witchcraft have been known in history. He lifts "a pious moan that the reign of the Lord's ministers in New England was now apparently further off than ever." De Forest continues:

Let all future Cotton Mathers learn charity from his unintentional sins, and the mortifying inevitable manner in which they found him out. For, if there is any lesson to be drawn from this book, it is that even in such a trinity as faith, hope, and charity, the greatest and most beautiful thing of all is charity. (Chap. 10, p. 404)

Not unlike his contemporary, Nathaniel Hawthorne, De Forest struggled with a moral problem which persistently asked the question of his readers: "Is it possible for sin, e.g., the 'unintentional sins' of a Cotton Mather, to be in any manner a path for progress of the human soul?" As a puritan born and bred but one evolved as a different species by reason of education and travel, De Forest was much engrossed with this question; and what is said, explicitly and implicitly, in *Witching Times*, indicates a cautious affirmative, if set in the perspective of his own century. What he might have said about the era of the late and unlamented junior senator from Wisconsin, the era of the five-star general, the era of the great society and assassins, is fascinating to speculate upon; yet, De Forest had summoned up the incubus Titus Oates and so perhaps we *know* what he would have said.

With *Miss Ravenel's Conversion from Secession to Loyalty*, De Forest presented to the American reading public a diorama of life and action never before seen, much less attempted, in the pages of fiction. Peace and war, graft, politics, and public life, privation and courage, fidelity and infidelity, social amelioration and disintegration, Southern "gentlemen" and Northern loyalists, all these subjects and many more, framed within the third assault on the American ideal, occupied De Forest's energy and artistry. The result was worthy of comparison with Stendhal's *The Charterhouse of Parma* (1839), and there can be little doubt that De Forest knew this novel and had it in mind.

Brigadier General John Carter's role of land shark in the novel is closely related to the notion of secession and loyalty. The pattern worked out is a complicated one but clear and logical. As the story opens, Lillie Ravenel is a political secessionist; she is a supporter of the Confederate cause despite her father's Unionist sympathies. She is a deserter from a cause equally important, according to De Forest—the moral cause; Carter's sudden appearance in the stuffy, but none the less correct, atmosphere of

New Boston (read New Haven) is notable because it is the beginning of Lillie's moral secession. She cannot resist this handsome, high-living, dashing *bon vivant*, this is most fascinating and best portrayed of all the sharks, this former professional army officer and ex-filibusterer, once-before-married and debt-ridden. He spirits Lillie away into a moral secession. Carter is her evil genius. This is not to overspeak for him, for he can excite renunciation in this young girl.

He is a strange mixture of military officer, whoremonger, lover, husband, politician, and adventurer. His great tragedy is that he possessed a tremendous capacity for good and for constructive works; however, his life was such that he never realized them. He was loyal to his profession, proud of his rank, brave, zealous, skillful in battle, tender (to his wife), virile, capable of absorbing punishment, gracious, sociable; in short, he was very much the man, such a one as was never seen in the American novel prior to 1867. De Forest is right in saying that under different circumstances, but certainly not during a civil war, Carter might have been a St. Vincent de Paul. Indeed, he had a sense of service in him, albeit a twisted one. His death in battle has an infallible logic to it. Mortally wounded, he lies on the battlefield. A chaplain asks him, "Have you thought of the sacrifice of Jesus Christ?" Carter sternly looks at him and tells him, "Don't bother!—where is the brigade?" To recall the words from *Seacliff*: Carter has returned for "safety" to his "own place."

By comparison, Edward Colburne, whom Lillie eventually marries, is a dull fellow when first met but a better man when well known. A young lawyer, a Yale graduate, he is conservative, cautious, and temperate in act and thought; his impeccable moral beliefs and tastes can never appeal to young Lillie. Once, however, he joins the army, his maturation as a man is a steady process. He becomes a splendidly resourceful and brave officer under Carter. His fighting qualities are derived from his intense loyalty to a political idea: reunion of the states. His baptism of fire, in battles similar to those De Forest himself survived, makes him fearless and courageous; he never wavers in his political loyalty or his moral loyalty. When he is mustered out of service in New Boston he is whole and complete, his ordeal of fire and agony at an end. In him the reader sees, in no uncertain terms (and strong terms for 1867), exactly what war does to a man. Colburne unburdens himself to Doctor Ravenel:

A soldier's life cultivates some of the Christian virtues; especially resignation and obedience. . . . You no more pretend to reason concerning your duties than a millstone troubles itself to understand the cause of its revolutions. You are set in motion and you move. . . . You obey because you are ordered. Oh, a man learns a vast deal of stoical virtue in field service. . . . The school of suffering teaches grand lessons. (p. 487)

His intense loyalty is to bring Lillie Ravenel Carter full circle with her marriage to him. Having begun her life in New Boston as a Secessionist, having changed to a Unionist while Carter's wife but a secessionist in the moral sense, she is now a loyalist, politically and morally. It is clear, is it not, that the long and oft disparaged title of the novel is, after all, precise and accurate? Yet, rich with ambiguity. De Forest was proud of his Colburne. "He is the soldier-citizen," he writes; "it is in millions of such men that the strength of the Republic consists." (p. 521) There is nothing ambiguous about him.

If Carter was new to the pages of the American novel so was his wife and lover, the title-lady. She is not beautiful, she is not too intelligent, and she is foolishly stubborn; she borders on being (or becoming) a prattling simpleton; her emotions and "beliefs" are no deeper than the skin on the back of her lovely hand. It is with her sudden marriage to Carter that she begins to grow up. She is no longer the teen-age child; she is now Lillie Ravenel Carter, the woman, the war bride, married to the one passion of her life. She is never to love with such abandon again. She is no prop or piece of furniture in the novel. She comes to know war; she lives in New

Orleans, an occupied city; she is involved in the Reconstruction when she teaches the Negroes on the plantation how to read and write. She is not by any means altogether sorry for her moral secession; for a brief moment she has known passion and happiness, for her first marriage plumbed deeps of pleasure she had never known and would never know with Colburne.

Miss Ravenel's Conversion from Secession to Loyalty is not only a realistic triumph, but is also an artistic triumph. Sadly, it failed utterly in the postwar market and attracted little attention. Maybe the public was tired of reading about the war; four years of it—enough. There seems to be no other reason, unfortunately for De Forest; fortunately, he had produced his masterpiece. He never attained to this level of achievement again; like many American novelists he is, for critical and aesthetic purposes—and I am speaking of literary realism, too—a "one-novel writer." For *Kate Beaumont* (1872, serialized, 1871) is fatally flawed; it is too long, the action is too contrived and too insistent, there are too many characters (the hero and heroine are pushed into the background by a gallery of very fine minor figures), and it is without direction and satisfying resolution. It has been badly overrated by critics. Yet the tale moves and says things of importance along the way, some of which have been alluded to in the brief discussion of "The High-Toned Gentlemen."

The problem can be stated simply: it is one of structure. But the work is not a loss. There is the vestige of the land shark theme in the person of Randolph Armitage, more of a descendant of Somerville in *Seacliff* than Carter in *Miss Ravenel*, for Armitage does not possess anywhere near the courage and honor of Carter. He has come into the midst of the Beaumont clan from the sinister "Dark Corner" of South Carolina, and wrecked Nellie's happiness (in the process of which De Forest dares to print some rather astonishingly frank details regarding a dismal marriage), he kills the knightly Colonel John Kershaw and then is driven off, to leave behind him Peyton and his children to piece together, paste together, really, the remnants. He is later killed in a fight in the same "Dark Corner." Although free of him maritally, Nellie will never be free of the scars, mental and physical.

There is the feudal code *duello* which De Forest would have us believe, and correctly, apparently, enslaved the South Carolinians as much as the economic code enslaved the Negro. The code *duello* is omnipotent; it is ubiquitous; it is lethal and deadly. De Forest can rend it with satire; he can weep over it, good moral gentleman that he is. His insistent preoccupation is an attempt to make himself understand this tragic waste of human potential in the semifeudal South; on the other hand, he says to his readers, and to himself again, that these prideful gentlemen lived by something, stupid as it was, beyond the ken of the ordinary mortal, beyond the worldly scheme of things: personal honor.

But to put aside this personal honor. We are then made aware that in *Kate Beaumont* the prime, inherent evil of the South is slavery, that second assault on the ideal. It is this institution that promotes sluggish minds and sluggish bodies and gives the aristocracy the idleness with which to provoke mischief. It is this institution which could produce a Poinsett Beaumont, a lawyer graduated from the university at Berlin but who has never had a case and does not want one, or a Vincent Beaumont, a physician graduated from Paris, again with no practice. De Forest hated slavery but he does not preach against it. The work is not, blessedly, an abolitionist tract. De Forest does not send a message. He accepts slavery as an inevitable social force.

Not by any means is he suggesting that this idleness and waste be seriously considered, much less salvaged. No (and he reminds us again of his own ambivalent attitude toward the "Southron," because of his own family connections), he fervently hopes that the "better peculiarities" of these "high-toned gentlemen" can be salvaged from the madness that had been slavery. The resultant ideal figure would be someone like Colonel John Kershaw, *beau ideal*, the patriarch of the Beaumont menage, the incarnation of Bayard south of the Mason-Dixon Line.

He was one of those simple, pure, honorable, sensible country gentlemen (of whom one meets more perhaps in our Southern states than in most other portions of this planet) who strike one as having a reserve of moral and intellectual power too great for their chances of action, and who lead one to trust that Washingtons will still be forthcoming when their country needs [them]. (p. 44)

Shot down and mortally wounded in a fresh outbreak of the feud between the Beaumonts and the McAlisters, the old colonel (who had fought in the War of 1812) makes the hot-headed Peyton Beaumont promise not to avenge him.

We South-Carolinians are not a law-abiding people. . . . We take punishment into our own hands. We cannot wait for the law. We do not trust the law. We make of ourselves judge, jury, and executioner. The consequence is that the State is full of homicide. It is wrong, Beaumont. It is a violation of the faith of man in man. It strikes at the base of society. It tends to barbarism. (p. 138)

In such a one lay not only the hope of the South (in the novel as well as in history) but also the hope of the nation (in the chaos of the Gilded Age). His death eventually terminates the feud.

Another significance is given Kershaw in *Kate Beaumont*, when one remembers that it was published in 1872, a time (as already mentioned several times) when political and moral structures in the United States were beginning to crumble. The guardians of public and private morality must call on the finer members and the finer aspects, viz., Kershaw, for effective and corrective action. If not, the "gentlemen of democracy" will engulf everything and everyone.

So we arrive at De Forest's final "chapter" in his "Great American Novel": the political novels, *Honest John Vane* and *Playing the Mischief*.

The "high-toned" elite was needed not only in Washington but also in the administration of the Reconstruction which, in De Forest's opinion (and he spoke as one who had partaken in it in Greenville, South Carolina), had partially achieved results; this elite was needed to ward off the assault by the gluttonous politicians feasting away in what V. L. Parrington once brilliantly called the Great Barbecue. The stage seemed set for their propitious entrance. On the stage, however, from the dark wings of the town of Slowburgh, and elsewhere, came an unexampled band of land sharks led by Honest John Vane, Darius Dorman, and Simon Sharp: the politician, the manipulator, the lobbyist, and the grafter, one more predatory than the other.

By all criteria, this *was* the final assault.

Maddened almost beyond reason to behold these "gentlemen of democracy" center stage, De Forest launched a counter-attack in *Honest John Vane* and *Playing the Mischief*. Never was an era to endure such pitiless, merciless satire. The efforts of Henry Adams and John Hay are ladylike in comparison. It is only fair to admit that *Vane* is a tract more than a novel. Its action serves as a skeleton on which De Forest drapes his indignant pronouncements on graft, corruption, and the ineptitude of the electorate. Wisely, he makes it very short and compact, for one can listen to a sermon just so long. Only twenty-four chapters long, it is his shortest novel.

While De Forest does regard Vane with contempt (he is the central character; the other "characters" are too one-dimensional to be bothered with), he does not completely shatter him; however, he lashes him unmercifully for his absolute unfitness for governmental responsibility. There is some basic good in the man, but when he begins to connive with Sharp and Dorman in the Great Subfluvial Tunnel Road, envisioned as running beneath the Mississippi and uniting Lake Superior with the Gulf of Mexico, a kind of below-ground Credit Mobilier project, that goodness is drowned.

Here is Honest John shortly after his election to the House:

He was too ignorant to be a professor in the State university, or even a teacher in one of the city schools; but it was presumed that he would answer well enough as a lawgiver for a complicated republic. (p. 46)

Here is Dishonest John, now a henchman of the Tunnel scheme:

There is a rabble in morals as well as in manners, and to this spiritual mobocracy Vane belonged by birth. . . . He did not prize virtue for its own sake, but because the name of it had brought him honor. . . . He had risen somewhat above his starting-point, but he still remained below the highest tide-water mark of vice, and got no foothold on the dry land of the loftier moral motives. (pp. 157–58, 174–75)

Following his extrication from the tentacles of the committee investigating the Subfluvial, Dishonest John asserts that *other* congressmen will have to depart Washington. Darius Dorman cynically disagrees.

I can tell you exactly how this thing is sure to come out. There will be a one-legged report. . . . As soon as it appears a debate will be arranged. All the old war-horses will gallop up and down among the charges. . . . When the dust clears away, it will be found that nobody is expelled. (p. 254)

He is correct. And Honest John becomes Weathercock Vane.

De Forest shudders visibly over such troglodytes manipulating government. And, understandably enough, they escape. But let it be understood that De Forest blames the great American people, the unwashed, equally, for sending an Honest John Vane to the Capital.

In this novel De Forest allows himself his first real opportunity for ejecting his long pent-up hatred of corruption and dishonesty. His haste is breathless as if he is fearful of not getting down all before it escapes him. His cynicism is not that of a callow radical but of a seasoned man of culture, an historian (something generally overlooked), and an observer of the national scene. His theories are old-fashioned, for the times, and hopelessly impractical. His aristocrats, his well-educated politicians, his well-behaved and well-informed press, his enlightened electorate, his honest voters and solons, his revenue tariff, his distrust of the large capitalistic monopolies, his concern for the farmer and for the laborer, his belief in the machinery of government as set up in the Constitution and not as operated by political bosses, all these people and beliefs, and many more, are doomed in *Honest John Vane* as they were pretty well doomed in public life in the 1870's.

Surely, so much had De Forest loosed his wrath that he would seem to have been exhausted, but he was to return, with a new band of land sharks, in *Playing the Mischief*. He begins more calmly; he writes more of a novel and less of a tract concerning the young, pretty widow, Josephine Murray, as she pursues her claim, dating from the War of 1812, against the federal government; and concerning the Honorable George W. Hollowbread, M.C., who will help Josie, now that he is enamored of her, to bag one hundred thousand dollars for her family's late and much lamented barn. Unlike *Honest John Vane*, which lacks minor characters, *Playing the Mischief* is crowded with them; and they push and shove each other for a place in De Forest's pitiless sun.

Josie Murray is his triumphant picturization of evil in Washington. Nothing hinders her progress. No man is too high or too low not to be used and sloughed off. No governmental function or body is sacred to her, and she can also use Sykes Drummond, M.C., a blood-brother to all the spoilsmen, who regards bribery as a normal function of life—or, at the very least, politics. He once remonstrates (to whom?):

I tell you, Mrs. Murray, that this state is rottener than Denmark. Well, there is one comfort, it gives *us* a chance. If George Washington's Congress of old-style, high-stepping country notables was sitting now, you and I couldn't get our claims through. (p. 72)

Josie can use the contemptible Jake Pike, the congressional agent and ex-congressman, never once reflecting, as De Forest does for her, "This is the fruit that universal suffrage bears when the industrious and virtuous cease to care for politics." (p. 154)

Finally, De Forest has stated the fault: universal suffrage; and here in full view is displayed the aristocratic paternalism first broached in *The Wetherel Affair*, bolstered this time by a remark by Colonel Julian Murray, USA, a high-minded officer in the tradition of Colonel Kershaw, to his brother, John:

We belong to honorable professions. I often think that matters could not have gone very badly in those old-time societies which were ruled by soldiers and priests. (p. 134)

The society in *Playing the Mischief* is certainly not "old-time," and it is ruled by land sharks. Josie Murray is the female of the species. She is the "girl of the period." She is, literally, the nation in the 1870's. Josie *is* democracy. What makes De Forest the absolute abjurer is that none of the sharks' victims is at all sympathetic; each is a weakling, a fool, or a brute; and each has within him potentialities to become a shark.

It should be apparent that the same hatred for spoliation, graft, corruption, and wire-pulling so active in *Honest John Vane* is present in *Playing the Mischief*. But De Forest's satire was mild in *Vane*. Here, in *Mischief*, he goes almost out of his senses with rage and frustration as he views this final assault by the political land sharks. He so loses control that he must expose every foible, weakness, and defect in his characters. He spares no one. Such a dispersion of fire, such a dispersal of thrusts, expose a serious lack of discipline. De Forest, once he has painted in his characters, simply cannot let his brush rest on the palette; he must brush in more and more contempt. However, by dabbing in touches of sardonic and bitter humor, he manages to retain sufficient command of his materials and emotions to execute his purposes. In superb comic scenes like Hollowbread's struggling with the hackdriver in the rain, or Jeremiah Drinkwater's false swearing to an affidavit, or Hollowbread's encountering the drunken Pickens Rigdon in a rural tavern, De Forest indicates his brotherhood with Dickens, even though it is a humor built on despair and loathing of the human race.

"The Great American Novel" ends here. Oh, there were other books, e.g., *Justine's Lovers* (1878), *Irene the Missionary*, *The Bloody Chasm*, and *A Lover's Revolt*. To be kind, they are not of moment. De Forest's career ends here, too. A good deal of his time in his later years was spent in bitterness, trying to determine, to fathom, the reasons for his eclipse and his neglect which came to him in the 1880's. One has but to read his letters to William Dean Howells to know how deep was this bitterness, to know the extent of his rancor at being ignored by the critics and gentlemen of letters.

In 1901, in the preface of *The Downing Legends*, De Forest addresses a few words to such a public, and although what he has to say refers specifically to the poems in the volume, his words can be applied to the whole of his work:

These adventures will no doubt be stigmatized by critic Gradgrind as incredible, unpractical and absurd. From his judgment I appeal confidently, like any other author, to remote posterity.

Good old Mr. Feeble Mind (well known to admirers of Bunyan) will also have somewhat to say, which will not be clearly understood, and so need not be answered, at least not prophetically.

Charles Chesnutt and the Color Line

ROBERT M. FARNSWORTH

In March 1889, Charles Chesnutt wrote to George Washington Cable: "It seems to me that there is a growing demand for literature dealing with the Negro, and for information concerning subjects with which he is in any manner connected—his progress in various parts of the world—in the U.S., in Brazil, in S.A., and in other lands. The opening up of Africa—it seems to me that these subjects would open up a vast field for literary work, and one in which a writer who was connected with these people by ties of blood and still stronger ties of sympathy, could be *facile princeps*, other things, being equal, or in which such a writer could at least earn a livelihood."

When he wrote this, Charles Chesnutt was thirty-one. He had published several stories, some in the *Atlantic*, and he had just finished a novella which was rejected, but which was a few years later to be rewritten, expanded, and published as his first novel, *The House Behind the Cedars*. Chesnutt was prudently feeling his way. Cable was useful in many ways. He was sympathetic on the race question, although the prudential Chesnutt felt some issues much more strongly than the supposedly radical Cable simply by virtue of Chesnutt's being a Negro. But Cable was a genteel writer who nevertheless was acutely aware of current Southern political and social affairs and could use the folklore of his region tellingly. Thus, Chestnutt saw in him a kindred spirit, but one who was white and already successful.

Cable's encouragement and criticism meant much to Chesnutt, but he knew he had his own role to shape.

Chesnutt was a successful, if unhappy, teacher and principal in Fayetteville, North Carolina, before he gathered his small but growing family and moved them in 1889 to Cleveland where he had been born. He had taught himself shorthand with years of diligent effort to give himself an economic tool to free him and his family from the South. Once in Cleveland he also studied law and after passing the bar examination at the head of his class, he joined his two skills together in a very successful business of court reporting and copying legal records of all kinds.

Earning his keep by his pen, becoming a full-fledged author, was a recurrent dream, but he was uncertain of his audience. Racial prejudice was pervasive in American society and pseudoscientific explanations of Negro racial inferiority were commonly accepted. Paul Laurence Dunbar was having some success as a poet, but no Negro had as yet made much of a mark in fiction. In view of these circumstances, Chesnutt hesitated to move out from the increasingly secure and comfortable position his successful business career was winning him.

Ten years after his request for advice from Cable, in September 1899, he felt that he had saved sufficient money and that he had built a sufficient literary base for him to risk abandoning his business and give full time to writing. There followed a brief but very productive period. His first collection of short stories *The Conjure Woman* had just been published in March. *The Wife of His Youth and Other Stories of the Color Line* appeared in print that winter. *The House Behind the Cedars,* Chesnutt's first novel, was published in 1900, and *The Marrow of Tradition,* his most ambitious novel on racial problems in 1901. During this same period he also wrote a modestly successful biography of Frederick Douglass.

Howell's evaluation of Chesnutt as a short-story writer in the May 1900 *Atlantic* evidences Chesnutt's contemporary success and gives a very encouraging view of his future:

But it is right to add that these are the exceptional times, and that for far the greater part Mr. Chesnutt seems to know quite as well what he wants to do in a given case as Maupassant, or Tourguenief, or Mr. James, or Miss Jewett, or Miss Wilkins, in other cases, and has done it with an art of kindred quiet and force. . . . They [Chesnutt's stories] are new and fresh and strong as life always is and fable never is. . . .

Our own more universal interest in him arises from the more than promise he has given in a department of literature where Americans hold the foremost place. In this there is happily no color line; and if he has it in him to go forward on the way he has traced for himself, to be true to life as he has known it, to deny himself the glories of the cheap success which awaits the charlatan in fiction, one of the places at the top is open to him.

But Chesnutt's writing failed to bring substantial rewards and he returned to his business in the winter of 1901. Perhaps he was not persistent enough. Certainly many other writers survived more serious rebuffs from their audience than Chesnutt sustained, and still went on to realize their ambition and talent. But Chesnutt was suspicious of the time and place. When *The Marrow of Tradition* failed to win him a sizable audience and thus secure him a reasonable income from his writing, he returned to his business success, quietly, but not bitterly, certain that the time was not yet ripe for a Negro writer to win broad or even reasonable acceptance from a dominantly white American reading audience. On the occasion of his receiving the Spingarn Medal, July 3, 1928, he reflected on his own writing career:

My books were written, from one point of view, a generation too soon. There was no such demand then as there is now for books by and about colored people. And I was writing against the trend of public opinion on the race question at that particular time. And I had to sell my books chiefly to white readers. There were few colored book buyers.

At that time the Negro was inarticulate, I think I was the first man in the United States who shared his blood, to write serious fiction about the Negro. But in this later and happier, though yet far from perfect age, there are a number of colored men who write books, and still larger number of white men and women who write books about the Negro, who, if they do not write the Negro up at least seek to tell the truth about the conditions in which he lives, and the truth is in the Negro's favor.[1]

Whether Chesnutt's view of his own position in history is accurate or not is an interesting question to explore. At any rate the current interest in the cultural heritage of the black man in America is helping to make Chesnutt's fiction available once more,[2] and a contemporary review of his achievement seems in order.

Chesnutt's first book-length publication was a collection of plantation tales told by a fictional Uncle Julias under the general title of *The Conjure Woman*. The vogue for such stories following the bitterness of the Civil War cannot help but raise suspicions of the American reading public's interest in avoiding the sharper and more painful social issues of racial conflict in the Reconstruction South in favor of the anecdotal folk humor which seemed safely distant in time and subject matter. The Civil War was a traumatic American experience. The wounds were deep and the skin still sensitive. George W. Cable, Thomas Nelson Page, Harry Stillwell Edwards, Joel Chandler Harris, and even Mark Twain characteristically masked their comments on the race question by setting their stories in the pre-Civil War South and straining their comments through the consciousness of a folk character or characters.

Chesnutt's *conjure* stories were accepted as excellent in an already well-established genre. In retrospect one can find in them the steadily sardonic view of slavery that one might expect from a Negro writer as opposed to the more romantically tinged and sensationally moralistic views of his white contemporaries, but these stories ruffled no white feathers. They seemed to bring only chuckles of appreciation and gave their author a modest foothold on the literary scene.

The Wife of His Youth and Other Stories of the Color Line was a more daring publication, and Houghton Mifflin added this title to their publications list with a little more sceptical trepidation. Chesnutt was very conscious of the importance of this publication and took great care of the ordering of the stories in the volume, most of which had been published separately.

The title story had already won enthusiastic comment from several quarters,[3] so it seemed an obviously wise choice as the lead off story. But the nature of the story offers some interesting speculation on the reasons for its acceptability.

The story is set in Groveland, a not too difficult to decipher cognate for Cleveland, and the time is contemporary. It gives the reader a mildly mocking view inside the blue-veined society of a northern city. The protagonist of the story is faced with a dilemma of honor which has racial and historical overtones. He was married before the War to a slave woman much older and darker than he. She warned him that her master was about to sell him even though he was a free man. He fled. Her master sold her down the river in retribution, and the War immediately introduced such social confusion that there seemed no hope of their finding each other. The young man educated himself and achieved considerable social and economic success in Groveland. As the story begins he is the most eligible bachelor and leading member of the blue veins and he is about to propose to a very delectable, light young widow from Washington, D.C. At this moment the wife of his youth who has been persistently and faithfully searching for her husband for the last twenty-five years appears on the scene, but she does not recognize him. His dilemma: to recognize her despite their differences in age, education, and social achievement or to bury the past and marry the prize which would cap his personal success story. He puts the story in a hypothetical fashion to those in attendance at a ball in his home in honor of the young widow whom everyone expects to be his bride. The audience and he know there is only one honorable choice, and he leaves them with the wife of his youth.

It is hard to see how a dominantly white audience could take offence at such a story. It gives them a peek-in at the curious world of Northern Negro urban society. It reassures them that prejudice is characteristic of black and white alike. And finally a man who is beginning to be successful in suspiciously close to middle-class white terms is chastened by the ties of his slavery past. And it all is done in the name of honor.

Chesnutt, of course, did not deliberately play to the prejudices of his white audience. There are other stories in this volume which clearly challenge those prejudices much more directly than this story plays to them. But it is difficult not to suspect that his audience's pleasure in a story well told was reinforced by strongly ingrained social attitudes.

The next story "Her Virginia Mammy" is again contemporary and urban in setting. A beautiful young woman who knows nothing of her past other than that she was an orphan raised by very decent parents who once were successful but now have fallen upon hard times hesitates to marry a young doctor because he is from such an eminent New England family even though he too at present is poor. She is teaching a dancing class of young Negro girls of mixed hue. In weariness and frustration, she tells her story to the sympathetic mother of one of her pupils. It is an extraordinary coincidence, but this mother reassures the young girl with good evidence that she was present when the girl's parents, parents who were FFVs, were killed in a steamboat crash, and that she was indeed her Virginia mammy. But with some innuendo the reader and the young doctor both understand that the woman is herself the mother of the young girl, and we all become complicitous to the young girl's unknowing act of passing.

Clearly this is a more challenging theme, and one

which touches on a characteristic Chesnutt response to "the problem." Chesnutt himself was light enough to pass, and he identified as his own the problem of those living along the color line. His first novel, which he worked on for years with a very heavy emotional investment, *The House Behind the Cedars*, focused on the family complications of passing. In an article in the Boston *Transcript* not long after the publication of *The Wife of His Youth and Other Stories*, Chesnutt wrote:

The most powerful factor in achieving any result is the wish to bring it about. The only thing that ever succeeded in keeping two races apart when living on the same soil—the only true ground of caste—is religion, and, as has been alluded to in the case of the Jews, this is only superficially successful. The colored people are the same as the whites in religion; they have the same standards and methods of culture, the same ideals, and the presence of the successful white race as a constant incentive to their ambition. The ultimate result is not difficult to foresee. The races will be quite as effectively amalgamated by lightening the Negroes as they would be by darkening the whites.

The *Transcript* article aroused hostile reaction in the press, but the thesis in "Her Virginia Mammy" was apparently hidden deftly enough that it brought no special notice.

The third story in the collection, "The Sheriff's Children," however, did provoke indignant reaction. Nancy Huston Banks, reviewing *The Wife* . . . for the *Bookman*, wrote,

To Mr. Chesnutt, then, may perhaps be given the credit of the first publication of a subtle psychological study of the negro's spiritual nature, the first actual revelation of those secret depths of the dusky soul which no white writer might hope to approach through his own intuition . . .

All this and more may be said in praise of the first and shortest of the nine stories forming the volume. The others are hardly worthy of mention in comparison with the first . . .

As fiction it [the volume] has little if any claim to consideration, and a graver fault than its lack of literary quality is its careless approach to the all but unapproachable ground of sentimental relations between the black race and the white race. Touching this and still more dangerous and darker race problems, Mr. Chesnutt shows a lamentable lack of tact of a kindred sort, an incomprehensible want of the good taste and dignified reserve which characterizes his first beautiful story and the greater part of all his work. "The Sheriff's Children" furnishes, perhaps, the most shocking instance of his reckless disregard of matters respected by more experienced writers.

"The Sheriff's Children" tells of a brave Southern sheriff bent on protecting a cringing Negro from the fury of a lynch mob. However, after the mob is braved and turned back, the Negro has changed also. He has stolen the sheriff's gun and now threatens him with deliberate and murderous fury as he reveals that he is the sheriff's own son, sold by him before the War. The sheriff had always regretted the deed, but had done nothing, and his son's just hatred sears him. But he is saved by his white daughter's intervention. After a sleepless conscience-ridden night, he finds his son a suicide in the morning.

This story has all the bold protest melodrama of Richard Wright or James Baldwin. There is no softening of the edges. White guilt is boldly proclaimed. One has to go back to pre-Civil War abolitionist fiction to find anything like it. But otherwise it is the first of its type written by an American Negro.

Following "The Sheriff's Children" we return to the blue vein society of Groveland in "A Matter of Principle," a story which mocks the racial prejudice within the Negro community even more sardonically than "The Wife of His Youth." Thus Chesnutt retreats to a safe subject after testing his white audience's sense of social justice. The pattern seems deliberate since it is repeated in the remaining five stories of the collection.

"The Web of Circumstance" is the only other strong protest story in the collection, and it is the ninth story coming appropriately at the end of the volume. "The

Passing of Grandison" (the sixth story) ridicules the white pretense to know and understand the Negro in such broad humor that it too may be considered a protest story, but each of these are preceded by two stories carefully calculated to be less offensive to the imagination of the white reading audience.

The reception of *The Wife of His Youth* encouraged Chesnutt in his belief that he could speak his piece as an American Negro and demonstrate his talent as an author of narrative fiction at the same time. And when the publishers began to vie to publish his long and carefully nurtured story of Rena Walden, the silver lining in the clouds seemed almost dazzlingly bright. The story of Rena was published as *The House Behind the Cedars*. It is a story of a beautiful and very light young girl who in the beginning is absorbed in the provincial world of a small Southern town and the care of an aging Negro mother. The girl's brother has secretly passed and become a successful Southern citizen in a neighboring state. When he surreptitiously visits his home and sees his sister's splendid beauty, he persuades his mother to let him take her to offer her all the advantages of his wealth and white associations. Rena makes a triumphant entry into the white world and becomes engaged to an appropriately handsome and promising young man when her mother's illness triggers a series of events which leads her fiancé to uncover the facts of her racial heritage. Rena bravely renounces the deception, sadly recognizing that her lover's passion is not strong enough to overcome the repugnance instilled in him by racial prejudice. She finally dies acknowledging that a faithful black childhood friend has loved her best.

Chesnutt wrote to a Mr. Robins at Houghton Mifflin concerning his hopes for the circulation of *The House Behind the Cedars*:

In the Washington, D.C. *Times* of August 18, 1900, was published a long editorial under the head of "The Yellow Peril in the United States," in which the writer said that the white race was becomming insidiously and to a large extent unknowingly corrupted with Negro blood, and cited a number of well-known Americans who are well-known, under the rose, to have remote Negro ancestry; of course, he did not mention names, but his descriptions were easily recognized by the well-informed. The question of "miscegenation" was brought up at the recent conference of leading white men of the South who met in May at Montgomery, Alabama, to discuss the race problem; and one of the solutions put forth involved the future amalgamation with the white race of at least a remnant of the black population. So that the subject I think may be regarded as generally opened up for discussion, and inferentially for literary treatment. I choose it because I understand it, and am deeply interested in it, but I hope to make it interesting to others because of the element of human interest involved.[4]

Chesnutt's first novel was a modest success, but it did not win him the large audience or the substantial literary income he was hoping for. Meanwhile social events weighed more and more heavily on Chesnutt's mind. There had been a savage race riot in Wilmington during the November elections of 1898. Reactionary white Southern politicians were gaining strength and victories in their movement to disfranchise the Negro voter of the South. Booker T. Washington's effort to win white support by playing down the resistance to these disfranchising efforts provoked heated argument in Negro communities throughout the nation. Chesnutt felt strongly and argued consistently with Washington on the disfranchising question, although he always dissented from the sharp personal attacks of such contemporaries as W. E. B. Dubois or Monroe Trotter.

The Marrow of Tradition is related to *The House Behind the Cedars* in somewhat the same fashion as "The Sheriff's Children" is related to "The Wife of His Youth." It clearly has much greater social bite. It challenges the white reading audience on an issue of social concern which leaves them no easy way out. The story focuses on a leading white family of a Southern town. Major Carteret has married wealth and is restoring his family's prestige by making the local newspaper an effective political instrument attacking the Reconstruction politics of the Republicans and Negroes. His wife has seemed barren until in late middle age she conceives a son upon whom the Major centers all his dreams for the restoration of his family. But from the beginning Chesnutt suggests a family and racial complication. The Major's wife's father had secretly married his Negro housekeeper shortly after the War. They had a daughter who resembles Mrs. Carteret strikingly. This daughter marries a very talented and socially dedicated young Negro doctor—I suspect the first New Negro in fiction—and they have a very healthy son. They also have purchased the old Carteret mansion.

The complications of guilt and injustice to the Negro members of the same family are interwoven into the political events of the novel to suggest an overriding sense of racial and family tragedy premonitory of Faulkner. However, Chesnutt makes his Negro figure melodramatically heroic in the manner of Harriet Beecher Stowe by having him eventually heed the pleas of the Carterets to use his surgical skill to save the life of their child even though his own has been murdered by a stray shot in a race riot ignited by the Major's newspaper's inflammatory distortion of racial news.

Chesnutt's ambition for this novel, however, was not restricted to a more militant racial challenge. The novel is his most ambitious effort at plotting. Besides the family complications of the Carterets indicated above and the social history which culminates in a race riot, Chesnutt also weaves in a love triangle dealing with Mrs. Carteret's young sister, the ne'er-do-well scion of a very honorable family, and an earnest young Quaker. More peripheral, but more interesting, is the personal story of racial vengeance of a strapping black, Josh Green, whose mother was made an idiot by the racial cruelty of a KKK visit. Green leads the blacks in a brave but desperate defensive effort against the whites and finally sinks his knife in the heart of the man who led the original KKK attack.

Chesnutt staked much on this novel. He wrote to his daughter Ethel: "You must join me in hopes for the success of my book, for upon its reception will depend in some measure whether I shall write, for the present, any more 'Afro-American' novels; for a man must live and consider his family." However, even as he wrote this, Chesnutt had once again resumed his business activity. It was almost as if he knew the verdict in advance or as if he were weary of the emotional effort needed to stand publicly against the sweep of social events. Chesnutt sent his book to several members of Congress as a possible antidote to the racial poison of Thomas Dixon's *The Leopard's Spots* which was then having a sordid vogue. Booker T. Washington aided and encouraged him in the effort. But the acceptance of disfranchising legislation, the assassination of McKinley and the public furore over Roosevelt's invitation to Washington to dine with him at the White House, and the increasing number of racial lynchings all suggested a disheartening climate for a Negro author driven by social imperatives emanating from his sense of racial injustice and drawn by his dream of literary eminence.

William Dean Howells had been one of Chesnutt's greatest literary supporters, and in other matters Howells had already demonstrated his social courage. Yet in Howells's review of *The Marrow of Tradition* one senses the sometimes Sunday School weakness of Howells's position. He does not attack the literary weakness of the novel where he could perhaps have been most helpful, but he suggests the grudging reluctance of the white audience to accept emotionally what it cannot in all conscience deny:

The Marrow of Tradition, like every thing else he has written, has to do with the relations of the blacks and whites, and in that republic of letters where all men are free and equal he stands up for his own people with a courage which has more justice than mercy in it. The book is, in fact, bitter, bitter. There is no reason in history why it should not be so, if wrong is to be repaid with hate, and yet it would be better if it was not so bitter. I am not saying that he is so inartistic as to play the advocate; whatever his minor foibles may be, he is an artist whom his step-brother Americans may well be proud of . . . No one who reads the book can deny that the case is presented with great power; or fail to recognize in the writer a portent of the sort of negro equality against which no series of hangings and burnings will finally avail.[5]

The Marrow of Tradition did not bring the income or acclaim Chesnutt hoped for and one senses that it was almost with relief that he returned to the relative peace and security of his business career. He became an increasingly solid and respected citizen of Cleveland and the nation. He actively supported worthwhile social organizations. He broke the color line on several exclusive social clubs. He lectured frequently. He travelled widely. He supported his family well. And he even now and then found time to write fiction. But essentially his literary career ended with *The Marrow of Tradition.*

His later novel *The Colonel's Dream* is not without interest, but it is an all-white novel with a message about the convict labor system in the South. It didn't raise his hopes nor disturb the tranquillity of the quiet success of Chesnutt's life. Chesnutt left the field to younger talent but was always ready with a helping hand and frequently a helping check.

Still it must have given him a reminiscent charge of emotion when he received a letter from Booker T. Washington dated February 28, 1905, saying: "In looking over our librarian's report for the last quarter, it may interest you to know that the two most popular books were 'The House Behind the Cedars' and the 'Marrow of Tradition' [*sic*]. Next came 'Ivanhoe' and 'David Copperfield.' "[6]

James Branch Cabell

FRED B. MILLETT

On January 6, 1920, John S. Sumner, Agent for the New York Society for the Suppression of Vice, signed an affidavit in the office of the District Attorney charging that Robert M. McBride and Company had published an "offensive, lewd, lascivious and indecent book." The book was James Branch Cabell's *Jurgen*. On January 14, 1920, the district attorney announced that a grand jury had brought in a true bill against the company, and, accordingly, that the case would be brought to trial. On the same day, Sumner, armed with a warrant, seized the plates and all the copies of *Jurgen* in McBride's offices.

For the suppression of *Jurgen*, Cabell should not have been completely unprepared. On December 28, 1918, Cabell had written to Burton Rascoe, one of his earliest enthusiasts and promoters, that Guy Holt, his editorial mentor at McBride's, "seemed pleased with the thing, in its not very readily decipherable state, but, to my honest surprise, considers its indecency out of all whooping. I am glad that he was spared the earlier version, which I believed I had toned down into quite harmless meanings perceptible solely to the evil-minded. Really I do not think the book as it stands contains a sentence unfit for utterance in any company; in fact, I know it does not." Before the publication of the book, there had been a long and friendly controversy between Cabell and Holt. Holt felt that the book should be called *Jurgen*; Cabell replied, "*Jurgen* does not content me, I cannot bring myself to believe it is the book's appropriate name, and upon customary bended knees I implore you to re-consider the repudiated *Pawnbroker's Shirt*." This contention, obviously, Holt won. There was more significant discussion as to what passages should or should not be excised to satisfy Holt's notions of literary decorum. At one time, Holt even suggested that McBride might publish an expurgated version for public consumption and an unexpurgated version privately. But on March 25, 1919, Cabell wrote Rascoe, "Your book is finally finished, unless Holt now develops qualms over its castrated decorum. He may. And, to be sure, *Jurgen* is vocal with Celtic echoes! You see, I began with a Russian framework, padded it out with pure Kiltartanese, flavored it with Graeco-Roman mythological scraps, and just for luck peppered it with a little Buddhistic lore. And do you know, now that *Jurgen* is complete, I think it very good? And not quite like anything with which I am acquainted." A little later, he wrote Holt, "Reading the book as a whole, I am naively pleased with it: I begin to think (which previously I did not think) that it is my best long story, and I find it, after all, autobiographical. In particular, I confess to being pleased with the numerous tiny changes made since you last saw the manuscript."

The suppression of *Jurgen* had both pleasant and unpleasant consequences for Cabell. In the first place, it made him a famous (or infamous) author. It also called the attention of curious readers to his earlier books. "My eleven preceding books, in this way, for the first time since I had begun writing books a bit over eighteen years earlier, reached more than a scant dozen or so attentive readers." It created an urgent demand for copies of *Jurgen* already in circulation and raised their price if they were obtainable. As late as December 1920, Zelda Fitzgerald wrote Cabell, enclosing a snapshot of herself, "For a very young and pretty girl, won't you *please* do an amazing favor? I simply have got to have a copy of *Jergen* [*sic*], and don't you know where I can find one? Its absence is spoiling a perfectly good Cabelliana—and anyway, I want to give it to Mr. F. Scott Fitzgerald for a Christmas present." On December 20, Cabell sent her a copy to give to "the most interesting young man that I know of anywhere." The suppression also led to Cabell's attracting admirers whom he found very trying. As he wrote years later in *As I Remember It*, "I did not enjoy being made notorious among the semi-illiterate as a purveyor of indecencies and a practitioner of all known iniquities. I disliked, and it may have been a trifle pee-vishly, the intrusive hordes of idiots and prurient fools, of busy-bodies, of unpublished authors well worthy of that condition, of dabblers in black magic, of catamites and amateur strumpets—all which delinquents and rab-ble and bobtail, Coolidge then being consul, hencefor-ward, for a full, fretful fifteen years or more, molested me and interfered with my opportunities to write in quiet." And, as he implies, his reputation for indecency, though unjustified, persisted. In the Author's Note that served as preface to the 1928 edition of *The High Place*, Cabell wrote, "The earliest of all reviews, I find, was in the *New York Times*. I record the judicious verdict of Mr. Lloyd Morris: 'This book is definitely distasteful in its explicit and gratuitous suggestion of sexual aberration and sexual perversion.' The *New York Tribune* helpfully suggested, in an editorial, that the then world-famous Leopold-Loeb murder had been prompted by a reading of *The High Place*. . . . And I find that even the very lateliest dated of the hundred or so reviews now in my scrap-book—by H. W. A. in the *Akron Press*—is regretta-bly of a piece with the others: '*The High Place* is an utterly impossible, sacrilegious, immoral and obscene work that could not be too strongly condemned.' "

The sequel to the suppression of *Jurgen* was anticli-mactic. The trial was first set for March 8, 1920, but the publisher's lawyers obtained a postponement. John Quinn, the distinguished lawyer and collector of modern books and manuscripts, was engaged, but from the start felt the case was hopeless. Ultimately he withdrew from it but collected a fee of a thousand dollars. Actually, the case did not come to trial until October 16, 1922. The lawyers for the Society for the Suppression of Vice presented its case; the company's lawyers moved for the direction of an acquittal. On October 19, Judge Charles C. Nott concluded his opinion by saying that "in my opinion the book is one of unusual literary merit and contains nothing obscene, lascivious, filthy, indecent or disgusting. The motion therefore is granted and the jury is advised to acquit the defendants."

And in these times of popular pornography how does *Jurgen* rate on the scale of indecency and lasciviousness? Although it is one of the most characteristic and the most distinguished of Cabell's books, on this particular scale it rates very low. Its hero, like many another Cabellian hero, indulges in a series of fornications, all in the interest of his quest for the perfection of feminine beauty, and there is what now looks like a rather juvenile and playful manipulation of phallic symbols, the sword, the spear, and other aggressive instruments. But the modern reader would find its indecencies, if he thought them indecencies, very modest and tepid indeed.

Jurgen is still the best known of Cabell's books, perhaps the only book of his at all known in this time. But it was not Cabell's only book, by any means. He was a compulsive writer. He said repeatedly that his purpose was "to write perfectly of beautiful happenings," and he also said, "The sole aim of my endless typewriting, in all the diverting while I have been about it, has been to divert, before any other person, me." His spirit seemed to call for uninterrupted diversion. In the memoir of his first wife, Priscilla Bradley Shepherd, in *As I Remember It*, he wrote that after her death "for the only time since I was as yet an undergraduate at college, the will to write had departed from me, and I lived rid of that milady which the learned term *cacoëthes scribendi*." Cabell insisted that his wife would "take a new book of his to bed, but presently she would turn off the light and go to sleep and never mention the book afterwards." In an interview she gave on an occasion when they were in New York, she told her questioner that "James is a perfectly normal man until after he has had his breakfast coffee and opened his mail. Then he goes upstairs, into his library to write his books." "If I really wanted to write books," Cabell says, "the woman meant to indulge me. . . . So I was permitted to have all to myself the library upstairs . . . and nobody upon any pretext was allowed to disturb me."

Under these favorable circumstances and evidently free from major financial pressures, Cabell was tremendously and ultimately perhaps injudiciously productive. His indefatigable productivity embraced, primarily novels and short stories, but also poetry, reminiscences, literary criticism, two important volumes of essays, *Beyond Life* and *Straws and Prayerbooks*, in which he outlined his aesthetic theory, not to mention three authoritative Southern genealogies published between 1907 and 1915. The Storisende Edition entitled *Biography of the Life of Manuel* which McBride published between 1927 and 1930 was made up of thoroughly revised versions of ten novels, five volumes of short stories, two volumes of essays and one volume of poetry. The latest book to be included in this edition was *The Way of Ecben*, 1929. Whether or not Cabell took numerology seriously, he liked to make his novels out of ten episodes and a volume out of ten short stories. He also grouped in threes his later writings, chiefly novels, under such headings as Their Lives and Letters, Virginians are Various, The Nightmare Has Triplets, Heirs and Assigns, and It Happened in Florida.

In whatever form Cabell wrote, he was—as he said repeatedly—antirealistic and pro-romantic. He was antirealistic, because he believed that what it is customary to call realism is not true to life, since it ignores man's capacity for dreaming of worlds and lives more rewarding and satisfying than those dull drab daily life offers. He also said that the themes that tie his books together are chivalry, gallantry, and poetry. By poetry, he meant the creative impulse that in whatever medium should be devoted to portraying lives more perfect than realism would allow. What Cabell failed to say and what led many readers astray was that his three major themes are all viewed ironically; so, if Cabell is a determined romanticist, his romanticism is constantly qualified by the incessant play of irony.

Cabell's major romantic symbol in the novels and short stories he included in the Storisende Edition is the French province of Poictesme, the imaginary province to which he gave surprising reality. In "A Note upon Poictesme," which introduces the illustrated edition of *The Silver Stallion*, he describes its origin. In one of the stories in *Gallantry*, John Bulmer, Duke of Ormskirk, first meets Mademoiselle de Paysange "in a byway of Louis Quinze's kingdom hitherto unknown to cartographers. For it was at this time . . . that Poictesme was born of an illicit union between Poictiers and Angoulesme. . . . It was then that the chateau of Bellegarde was erected, and the Forest of Acaire was planted." Gradually, other castles, towns, and natural features were added, and the end papers of *The Silver Stallion* are a detailed map of the fabled province.

Poictesme is a land of untold antiquity. The earliest records of the history of the province show that it was peopled not only by heroes and amazingly beautiful and obliging women but also by fallen gods from almost every known mythology, witches, wizards, and magicians of every kind, and animals and birds that had their origin in the most fantastic of medieval bestiaries. Poictesme endured, and furnished, in fact or imagination, the setting for the most significant actions of Cabell's major heroes, ancient and modern. *Biography of the Life of Manuel*, the title that Cabell gave the Storisende Edition, is not really redundant, for Cabell conceived the legendary Manuel as the ancestor of progeny who inherited many of his characteristics, who persisted into Cabell's own time and country, and whose genealogy he obligingly supplied in *The Lineage of Lichfield* (1922). (For this binding concept, one may conjecture, Cabell found his model in the serious work he did and the

publications he brought out on Southern genealogy.)
Characteristics of Manuel that recur in his male descendants are their impatience with the limitations of
domesticity and their desire to escape into more satisfying experiences. These feelings are intensified by their
search for perfection of beauty in woman, and toward
the attainment of this ideal their quests are directed. But
the almost obsessional pattern of Cabell's books usually
ends with his hero's return to domesticity with a renewed awareness of its reassurances and gratitude for
them.

The variations on this archetypal pattern may be sufficiently illustrated in the Storisende novels that seem
most deserving of attention: *The Cream of the Jest*
(1917), *Jurgen* (1919), *Figures of Earth* (1921), *The
High Place* (1923), *The Silver Stallion* (1926), and
Something About Eve (1927).

In *The Cream of the Jest*, the hero, Felix Kennaston,
one of the many masks that Cabell assumes, is a Southern gentleman, a successful author, and a moderately
happy married man. He is engaged on a romance of the
sort that Cabell was to write. To the characters in his
romance, he says, "It may well be that I, too, am only a
figment of some greater dream. . . . It may be the very
cream of the jest that my country is no more real than
Storisende." Kennaston is obsessed by the need to cap-
ture the perfect, the Platonic, beauty of Ettare, "that
ageless lovable and loving woman of whom all poets had
been granted fitful glimpses." The sigil of Scoteia, half
of a broken disc he finds in the garden, makes it possible
for him to go in quest of Ettare through the centuries.
He was at Troy when Priam was a boy playing marbles,
in Jerusalem on the day of the Crucifixion, and rode with
Ettare to the guillotine of the French Revolution. The
dream ends if and when he touches Ettare. Back in
Lichfield, he finds the other half of the sigil on his wife's
dressing table; it is part of the cover of a cosmetics jar.
"Many thousand husbands," he says, "may find at will
among their wives' possessions just such a talisman."

Jurgen, the hero of the novel of that name, is a fifty-year old pawnbroker, married to an infinitely exasperating wife, Dame Lisa. Encountering the Devil dressed as a monk, he happens to speak kindly to him and is granted a wish. His wish is to rid himself of his wife; the Devil grants his wish. But in Jurgen there stirs a feeling that he must recover her for fear of what the neighbors will say. So he is off on his quest. He meets the centaur Nessus who gives him a gleaming shirt, which restores his youth but also deprives him of the shadow that manifests his human reality. His quest characteristically involves him in a series of erotic encounters. The first is with Dorothy la Desirée, with whom he had long ago experienced a violent attack of calf love. She has almost forgotten him, and what she has become is Jurgen's first experience of disillusionment. He goes on to rescue Guinevere from her sleeping-beauty trance but tires of her and willingly turns her over to King Arthur. He spends some time with Anaitis, Queen of Cockaigne, who is expert in erotic subtleties. "Yet the deeper Jurgen investigated, the more certain it seemed to him that all such employment was a peculiarly unimaginative pursuit of happiness." He marries a Hamadryad. Ultimately, he reaches Helen of Troy, the perfection he has unconsciously been seeking. Here occurs one of the best scenes in the novel.

Jurgen stood at Queen Helen's bedside, watching her, for a long while. . . . And reflectively he drew back the robe of violet-colored wool, a little way. The breast of Queen Helen lay bare. And she did not move at all, but she smiled in her sleep.

Never had Jurgen imagined that any woman could be so beautiful nor so desirable as this woman, or that he could ever know such rapture. So Jurgen paused.

"Because," said Jurgen now, "It may be this woman has some fault: it may be there is some fleck in her beauty somewhere. And sooner than know that, I would prefer to retain my unreasonable dreams, and this longing which is unfed and hopeless, and the memory of tonight. Besides, if she were perfect in everything, how could I live any longer, who would have no more to desire? No, I would be betraying my own interests, either way; and injustice is always despicable."

So Jurgen sighed, and gently replaced the robe of violet-colored wool, and he returned to his Hamadryad.

Later, Jurgen descends into Hell and marries a vampire. Hell has been invented by Koshchei, the god of things-as-they-are, to satisfy prideful sinful man's demand for punishment. Then, with the aid of a boy who proves to be the innocent Jurgen of his youth, he ascends into Heaven. But he decides to avoid the part of Heaven where Steinvor, his grandmother, dwells. "'Yet I shall keep away from my grandmother, the Steinvor whom I knew and loved, and who loved me so blindly that this boy here is her notion of me. Yes, in mere fairness to her, I must keep away.' . . . and this was counted for righteousness in Jurgen." But the God of Jurgen's grandmother reports to him the circumstance that led to Koshchei's creation of Heaven.

Then Koshchei reflected. . . . "Where does this woman come from?"

"From Earth," they told him.

"Where is that?" he asked: and they explained to him as well as they could.

"Oh, yes, over that way," Koshchei interrupted. "I remember. Now—But what is your name, woman who wish to go to Heaven?"

"Steinvor, sir: and if you please I am rather in a hurry to be with my children again. You see, I have not seen any of them for a long while.". . .

"Do you tell me about your children," Koshchei then said to Steinvor: "and do you look at me as you talk, so that I may see your eyes."

So Steinvor talked of her children: and Koshchei, who made all things, listened very attentively. . . .

Then privately Koshchei asked, "Are these children and grandchildren of Steinvor such as she reports?"

"No, sir," they told him privately.

So, as Steinvor talked, Koshchei devised illusions . . . and created such children and grandchildren as she described. . . .

Then Koshchei bade her turn about. She obeyed: and Koshchei was forgotten.

Finally, Jurgen remembers that the initial purpose of his quest was the recovery of Dame Lisa; so he gives Koshchei the shirt that had restored his youth and in return gets Dame Lisa back, and that abused lady rewards Jurgen with the sort of scolding but understanding lecture to which the years have accustomed him.

Figures of Earth purports to give the history of how the swineherd Manuel by deeds of prowess conquered Poictesme, became its Count, and founded a line that persisted into twentieth-century Lichfield. The romance is not so much a variation on one of his major themes, chivalry, although this theme has its place, as Cabell's most elaborate treatment in fiction of the theme of poetry, the creation of imaginative works of arts. Manuel's quest, like Jurgen's, begins with his ridding himself of his tedious wife, the kitchen wench, Niafer. Confronted by a mysterious supernatural figure, Manuel consents to save his own life by turning Niafer over to the power of death. Again, as in *Jurgen*, Manuel's quest involves erotic encounters with a series of women: Suskind, Princess Alionora, whom he gives up so that she may marry the King of England, and—most important of all—Freydis, Queen of Audela. Because of her love for him, she becomes a mortal, and then she expresses explicitly the Platonism that is the ground for Cabell's concern with perfection. She says, "My lost realm alone is real. Here all is but a restless contention of shadows that pass presently; here all that is visible and all the colors known to men are shadows dimming the true colors, and time and death, the darkest shadows known to men, delude you with false seemings: for all such things as men hold incontestable, because they are apparent to sight and sense, are a weariful drifting of fogs that belie the world which is no longer mine." It is she also who teaches Manuel how to breath life into the images that he has made of clay but that fail to come up to his hopes when they move and have their being. He says, "Now I have seen the miracle: I know that it is possible for the man who has your favor to become as a god, creating life, and creating lovelier living beings than any god creates." Still he is not satisfied with what he has made. Nor is he any more pleased with his fellowworkmen.

He had thought it, he said, an admirable thing to make images that lived until he saw and considered the appearance of these habitual makers of images. They were an ugly and rickety, short-tempered tribe, said Manuel: they were shiftless, spiteful, untruthful, and in everyday affairs not far from imbecile: they plainly despised all persons who could not make images, and they apparently detested all those who could. With Manuel they were particularly high and mighty, assuring him that he was only a prosperous and affected pseudo-magician, and that the harm done by this self-styled thaumaturgist was apt to be very great indeed.

Finally, Manuel decides to accept his own death for the sake of recovering Niafer.

I suppose that if she were taken away from me again I would again be attempting to fetch her back. And I do not like to hurt the poor foolish heart of her, because she is always able to make me uncomfortable. . . . So I get through each day, somehow, by never listening very attentively to the interminable things she tells me about. But I often wonder, as I am sure all husbands wonder, why Heaven ever made a creature so tedious and so unreasonably dull of wit and so opinionated. And when I think that for the rest of time this creature is to be my companion I usually go out and kill somebody. Then I come back, because she knows the way I like my toast.

When he is summoned by Alianora, Queen of England, to assist her in the production of a male heir and Niafer is aware of the purpose of his departure, we have this interchange:

Dom Manuel laughed. "Dear snip," he said, "come, honestly now, what have you been meditating about while I talked nonsense?"

"Why, I was thinking I must remember to look over your

flannels the first thing tomorrow, Manuel, for everybody knows what that damp English climate is in autumn."

"My dearest," Manuel said, with grave conviction, "you are the archetype and flawless model of all wives."

At the end, when Manuel is summoned by Grandfather Death, Death asks him,

"What is that thing?". . .
"It is the figure of a man," said Manuel, "which I have modeled and remodeled, and cannot get exactly to my liking. So it is necessary that I keep laboring at it, until the figure is to my thinking and my desire."
Thus it was in the old days.

In *The High Place*, Cabell leaps across the ages to the very end of the seventeenth century and to Florian De Puysange, of the eighteenth generation of Manuel's descendants. When the tale begins, Florian is a boy of ten full of fairy-tale fantasies. He is haunted by a glimpse he had of a sleeping beauty Melior on an occasion when he penetrated to the High Place. Later, after he has already disposed of four wives by methods that resemble Bluebeard's and is about to marry again, he encounters Janicot, one of the numerous masks that Cabell gives the Devil, and, as a result of a bargain he makes with him, returns to the High Place, awakens Melior, woos her, and brings her back to Poictesme as his bride. She is accompanied by her spiritual advisor, Holy Hoprig. Through them, Florian hopes to achieve the possession of both beauty and holiness. "Here were perfect beauty and perfect holiness attained once by mankind, and in consequence not unattainable. To dream of these two had kept Florian prodigally supplied with lofty thoughts of human excellence." But both his hopes are unfulfilled. Melior deteriorates into a garrulous, illogical, and querulous woman. "He did not find that, as wives average, his Melior was especially loquacious: it was, rather, that when she discoursed at any length, with her bewildering air of commingled self-satisfaction and shrewdness, he could never make out quite clearly what she was talking about: and as went intelligence, his disenchanted princess seemed to him to rank somewhere between a magpie and a turnip." Florian's search for holiness in the person of Holy Hoprig likewise ends in disenchantment. At first, Florian regards him with reverence since his cult is popular in Poictesme. But then it turns out that he has come to be regarded as a saint only because he has been confused with a real saint, Horrig, from whose tomb the tail of the First R has fallen away. Hoprig is a libidinous priest of some pagan cult, and his behavior in Poictesme so disturbs Heaven that the Archangel Michael is sent down to dispose of him suitably. But it is Janicot who makes a proposal that satisfies the Archangel. "Let Hoprig and Melior and their child, too, return to Brunelois and to the old time before he was a saint. . . . And this Melior and this Hoprig will no longer be real persons, but will once more blend into an ancient legend of exceeding beauty and holiness." When their colloquy ends thus satisfactorily, the two faces—of the Archangel and Janicot— "somehow to lended into one face, and Florian knew that these two beings had melted into one person, and that this person was prodding him gently." The person is his father awakening the boy from the extraordinary dream that he has had. He thereupon gives the boy the fruit of his wisdom about life. "To submit is the great lesson. I too was once a dreamer: and in dreams there are lessons. But to submit, without dreaming any more, is the great lesson; to submit, without either understanding or repining, and without demanding of life too much of beauty or of holiness, and without shirking the fact that this universe is under no least bond ever to grant us, upon either side of the grave, our desires. To do that, my son, does not satisfy and probably will not ever satisfy a Puysange. But to do that is wisdom."

In *The Silver Stallion*, Cabell recounts the events that followed the disappearance of Manuel. The two major themes of the book are closely related. The first is the process by which the sensual brawling Manuel is transformed into a redeemer through the efforts of his pious wife, Niafer, and her spiritual advisor, Holmendis. They erect an imposing tomb to Manuel, though his body is missing, and adorn it with precious stones that prove to be imitations. Thanks to them, Manuel the Redeemer comes to be widely worshipped and influential. The second theme concerns the reactions to the transformation of Manuel and the ultimate fates of the nine champions who, under Manuel, had constituted the Fellowship of the Silver Stallion. Their attitudes range from more or less sturdy faith to vigorous unbelief; their fates are as various as their attitudes. For instance, a Sylan, Glaum-Without-Bones, turns Guivric into a phantom by taking possession of his body and, as a mortal, promptly becomes a convert to the worship of Manuel. Kerin so annoys his witch-wife Saraïde by banalities that he offers her in place of the one truth she is intent on knowing that she pitches him down a well. Underground, he discovers a collection of all the books in the world; he reads them all and, years later, having discovered the one truth, he returns to Saraïde, who has learned it, not from books but from life. "Time, like an old envious eunuch, must endlessly deface and maim, and make an end of, whatever anywhere was young and strong and beautiful, or even cozy. . . . Well, and Saraïde, as usual, was in the right! It was the summit of actual wisdom to treat the one thing which was wholly true as if it were not true at all."

Coth, the most ruffianly of the champions, refuses to believe in Manuel the Redeemer and sets off to find the real Manuel and bring him back to Poictesme. Ultimately, he finds him in the Place of the Dead, and is forced to accept reluctantly what Manuel has to say to him. "I have gone, forever. But another Manuel abides in Poictesme, and he is nourished by these fictions. Yearly he grows in stature, this Manuel who redeemed Poictesme from the harsh Northmen's oppression and lewd savagery. . . . It is this dear Redeemer whom Poictesme will love and emulate: men will be braver because this Manuel was so very brave; and men, in one or another moment of temptation, will refrain from folly because his wisdom was so well rewarded: and, at least now and then, a few men will refrain from baseness because all his living was stainless."

The novel ends appropriately with the meditations of Jurgen, Coth's son, at the tomb of Manuel. "You knew the shining thing to have been, also, the begetter of so much charity, and of forbearance, and of bravery, and of self-denial,—and of its devotees so strange, so troublingly incomprehensible, contentment, that it somewhat troubled Jurgen. . . . And Jurgen was wondering what it was that the child who Jurgen once had been had, actually, witnessed and heard upon Upper Morven. He could not now be certain: the fancies of a child are so unaccountable, so opulent in decorative additions. . . . And perhaps it was natural enough (in this truly curious world) that Jurgen nowadays should be the only person remaining in any place who was a bit dubious as to the testimony of that child."

Something about Eve plays several significant variations on the archetypal pattern of Cabell's earlier books. Its hero, Gerald Musgrave, an early nineteenth-century descendant of Manuel, is at work on a romantic poem about his famous ancestor. But he is not only dissatisfied by the poem but bored by the exigencies of his mistress, Evelyn Townsend. He escapes from the unsatisfactory poem and the trying mistress by accepting the offer of the Sylan, Glaum of the Haunting Eyes, to take his place as the poet and as Evelyn's lover. Musgrave sets out for Antan, the paradise of all great creative spirits. His boredom with sex makes it easy for him to deal with four supernatural variations on the personality of Evelyn and to cope decisively with Koleos Koleros, the female principle, and the Holy Nose, the male principle.

Musgrave wanders through the waste land of Lytreia (reality), the critical desert of Turoine (routine), but in the city of Caer Omn (romance) views in a gigantic mirror all his admired heroes from Prometheus and Odysseus down to Don Juan and Jurgen. But when he arrives at Mispec Moor (compromise), his desire to push on to Antan is frustrated by his succumbing to Maya of the Fair Breasts, who adorns him with rose-colored glasses, makes him physically comfortable, and supplies him with a son. So, there he dallies through the years and converses contentedly with the heroes passing on their way to Antan. He even engages in a long theological discussion with Jahveh, who, starting life as a Midianite storm god, was kidnapped by the Jews, and is now disconcerted to find himself a trinity. Ultimately, his own vision of Antan fades and he sees his son ride away in quest of his Antan. Musgrave returns to his study in Lichfield, an older and wiser man. He finds that, in his absence, Glaum has become a distinguished anthropologist specializing in the sexual customs of mankind. Musgrave dismisses Glaum, tears up the unfinished poem, and prepares to resume his relations with the now older and less exigent Evelyn.

Cabell, it might be argued, is less interesting as a writer qua writer than he is as a writer the vicissitudes of whose reputation offer challenging problems in the history of taste and of critical judgment. It is not too difficult to plot a graph of the rise and fall of his critical reputation. In the twenties, Cabell's most enthusiastic admirers expressed judgments that now seem fantastically extravagant. In the thirties, critics arrived at more considered and qualified judgments. Then, suddenly about 1940 there began a period of almost complete neglect: Despite the fact that Cabell went on writing till 1955 and lived till 1958, his writings got almost no attention except in ephemeral reviews. Then, the publication of Edmund Wilson's masterly essay, "The James Branch Cabell Case Reopened," which appeared in the *New Yorker* on April 21, 1956, pointed to Cabell as a writer deserving serious consideration and may very well have inspired the younger writers who have published books on Cabell in the sixties. In consequence, a nonidiosyncratic judgment of Cabell may now be possible.

The extravagant overpraise of the twenties came from

literary contemporaries of Cabell who were not only enthusiasts for his work but his personal friends. Although Cabell once expressed some concern lest his faithful publisher McBride should lose money on his books, he was much less concerned with the size of his royalties than with the number of his readers, and, as the correspondence in *Between Friends* (1962) makes clear, he used his influential admirers, once he had discovered them, with cool assiduity. He repaid them by dedicating either whole novels or portions of a novel to them and gave them the opportunity to write introductions to certain of his books when he was preparing them to appear in the Storisende edition of his works.[1]

Cabell's novels fed the twenties appetite for sophistication. They seemed to belong to the genre of such novels as Aldous Huxley's *Crome Yellow* (1921) and *Antic Hay* (1923) and Carl Van Vechten's *Peter Whiffle* (1922) and *The Blind Bow-Boy* (1923). As Cabell wrote in *These Restless Heads* (1932), "Oncoming antiquarians, I suspect, will not ever give us sophisticated writers of the 'twenties our due credit for the pains with which we learned to converse in drawing rooms about brothels and privies and homosexuality and syphilis and all other affairs which in our first youth were taboo,—and even as yet we who have reached fifty or thereabouts cannot thus discourse, I am afraid, without some visible effort. I have noted a certain paralytic stiffening of the features (such as a willing martyr might, being human, evince at the first sight of his stake,) which gave timely warning that the speaker was now about to approach the obscene with genial levity!"

The attempt to suppress *Jurgen* encouraged some of Cabell's most enthusiastic admirers to give the world their hearty endorsement of his writings. Hugh Walpole was one of the first to publicize the grounds for his high valuation of him. In 1921, he wrote, "No one travelling around the United States of America during these last months, no one at least who is interested in literature, can escape the persistent echo of Cabell's name. . . . I had not been in the United States for two weeks before someone said to me: 'Well, at any rate, there is Cabell.' That was a new name to me. I was given *Beyond Life* to read. My excitement during the discovery of that perverse and eloquent testament was one of the happiest moments of my American stay. . . . It is with these latest works—*The Cream of the Jest, Beyond Life,* and *Jurgen* that he has reached the full command of his talent. . . . With the single exception of Joseph Hergesheimer, I know of no three books by one and the same author written in the last ten years that have given me so vivid a sense of a new, definite, and genuine personality, whose arrival on the scene must have a definite impression upon English literature. . . . With the ending of Jurgen's chronicle, we can acclaim with no uncertain voice the definite arrival of a talent as original and satisfying as anything that our time has seen."

In 1921, also, Vernon L. Parrington contributed to the *Pacific Review* an essay, "The Incomparable Mr. Cabell," (reprinted posthumously in *The Beginnings of Critical Realism in America,* Volume III of his *Main Currents in American Thought*), which is the most searching essay written on Cabell in the twenties. Parrington begins his essay by saying, "The successive volumes of James Branch Cabell have provided the tribe of critical Jeffries with a rich vein of diversion. They have recognized no closed season in their full-lunged pursuit of the strange heirs of Mr. Cabell's invention, and such Homeric absurdities of comment have been flung at him, that he is in a fair way to become our classic example of the fatuousness of contemporary estimates. As whimsical as Bernard Shaw, as provocative as Chesterton, he is more incomprehensible than either to all readers who do not choose to like what they have not always liked." And he concludes his essay by saying, Cabell's cosmic irony "is the stuff of which great literature is made. And Mr. Cabell is creating great literature. A self-reliant intellectual, rich in the spoils of all literatures, one of the great masters of English prose, the supreme comic spirit thus far granted us, he stands apart from the throng of lesser American novelists, as Mark Twain stood apart, individual and incomparable."

In 1926, Joseph Warren Beach, in *The Outlook for American Prose* said of the style of Cabell's *Beyond Life* and *Straws and Prayerbooks*, "Mr. Cabell brings to the illustration of his romantic theory of literature such intellectual subtlety, such ripened culture, and a style so rich, suave, pointed, and original that he must be counted with assurance as one contemporary American who has produced criticism which is literature." In "The Holy Bottle" essay in the same volume, he made a close and detailed analysis of Cabell's style in his romances: "The flavor of elegant and playful bookishness, with its discreet, pervasive tincture of archaism, is particularly suited to the fundamental attitude of skeptical disillusionment from which Mr. Cabell proceeds," and again, "he is at one with all lovers of paradox, the Chestertons and Shaws, the Swifts and Frances—those subtle and lively thinkers in whom one thought begets another, assertion begets denial, denial assertion and ideas come to stand on their feet only when they are tired of standing on their heads. There is in him that mocking will-of-the-wisp spirit, 'now you have me and now you don't,' which is the delight of jesting Pilates, and a thorn in the flesh of those who are forever staying for an answer."

In 1927, H. L. Mencken paid tribute to a writer whose works he had championed. Cabell's "one aim in life," he wrote, "is to make himself a first-rate artist—and this aim, I am inclined to think, he has come nearer to realizing than any other American of his time." Of *Jurgen*, he said, "Where is there another American book so beautifully contrived, so genuinely a masterpiece? It will, I believe, long outlast its day. It is packed with the reflections of an immensely enterprising and original mind, and it is turned out with the virtuosity of an authentic artist," and finally, "Cabell knows how to write. If this Republic has ever produced a more accomplished performer upon the parts of speech, then I ask respectfully to be furnished with his name and address."

Carl Van Doren's *James Branch Cabell,* first published in 1925 and brought out in a revised edition in 1932, may be taken as summing up the extravagant esteem with which Cabell was regarded in the twenties. It is the only book exclusively devoted to Cabell until the proliferation of books about him in the sixties. Early in the book, Van Doren writes that it is not easy "to resist the temptation to say, at the outset, that Mr. Cabell is already a classic if any American novelist of this century is. The shifts of taste from age to age may now depress and now exalt the credit of the famous *Jurgen.* . . . Both by its wit and its beauty, *Jurgen* will survive." His novels "stand, graceful and compact, devoted to the record of beautiful happenings in a language which never falls below a high level of perfection. . . . There are no angles in his surfaces. His style purrs to a degree that now and then begets monotony; his phrases, ordinarily so felicitous, now and then have a mannered look; he so often avoids the simple way of saying simple things that he overloads his language. . . . At his best, however, and he is very frequently at his best in his short stories, he is crystal clear in his meanings, and delicately varied in his rhythms." Finally, Van Doren maintains that "there seems to be no longer any reasons for not associating him with the only comparable American romancers, Hawthorne and Melville. . . . Mr. Cabell, more systematic than Melville and Hawthorne in his thinking, is more thorough in his art. He has left behind his own place and his own age, and has taken refuge in an imagined realm where the very shadows are brighter than the sunshine of Virginia. He pays for this greater detachment with a certain rarefaction; Hawthorne is more solid, Melville more robust. It is in wit and loveliness that Mr. Cabell matches them."

In the thirties, the critical tone taken toward Cabell slowly changed. In 1934, Harry Hartwick, in *The Foreground of American Fiction,* though chiefly concerned with the naturalists, the realists, and the novelists whom he called humanists—Henry James, Edith Wharton, Willa Cather, and Thornton Wilder, devoted a short section, "Beyond Life," to early American expatriates, to Joseph Hergesheimer, and to Cabell. Hartwick, unlike Joseph Warren Beach, found his style especially irritating. "His Biography is written in a tricky, anachronistic prose . . . and suffers from an addiction to lingual and orthographic japes and symbolisms. . . . His narratives are decked out with romantic moonshine, scholastic hocus-pocus, and such pedantic words as siccative, ventripotent, and mundivagant. It is a kind of 'left-handed' style, that smells of the lamp and outworn masquerades." In the following year, Harlan Hatcher, on the other hand, in *Creating the Modern American Novel*, displayed an enthusiasm reminiscent of the twenties. "James Branch Cabell is one of the great satirists. . . . He has with the most urbane control of his irritations pricked at the eternal follies of all men everywhere in all ages. His keen and graceful mind has seldom failed to preserve its decorum, and a joyous wit has never been absent from his polished prose." It has been his "calling to remind prosaic men, in season and out, that they are creatures of moods: that beyond the rigid world of common-sense there is a pliant and controllable land of dreams: and that they ought to 'keep faith steadfastly with all those impossible things which are not true, but which ought to be true.' The novels . . . are unique in our literature, and they have contributed to the American novel a type without which it would be poorer and incomplete."

Arthur Hobson Quinn, on the broader canvas of his *American Fiction, as Historical and Critical Survey* (1936), gave a more censorious view of Cabell. His belated Victorian taste is evident in his shock at Cabell's account in *The Silver Stallion* of the transformation of the rake and ruffian Manuel into a redeemer by his pious widow Niafer and her spiritual advisor Holy Holmendis. "The parallelism of Manuel's career to that of Christ, beginning with his virgin birth and leading to his 'Eucharist' is offensive, of course, and in bad taste, but it is all the more inexcusable because it is dragged in. Cabell of course does not mention Christ, and he attempts to forestall criticism by a marshalling of characters to whom tradition has attached somewhat similar events." Moreover, Manuel's "resurrection rests upon an empty tomb and the unsupported word of the child, Jurgen, who, it is implied, had made up most of the story." (It is not surprising that the reviewer of Quinn's book in the World Telegram should wonder "what would happen at Pennsylvania if Professor Quinn, while lecturing on James Lane Allen, to whom he awards eleven pages, suddenly discovered that his students were surreptitiously reading James T. Farrell's chronicles of pilgrimages to the bathroom. The result might not be pleasant, and therefore hardly a theme to be approved for American fiction.") More broadly, Quinn felt that the one quality in Cabell's fiction that explains "the passing of his vogue" is his lack of sincerity, a charge that, like the assertion of a writer's sincerity, it is impossible to prove or disprove. There is, however, one literary gift for which Professor Quinn admired Cabell, namely the gift of style. "He has not much of a story to tell, but he has the gift, especially in his early work, of the well-chosen word, the charming phrase, and the sentence whose proportions are a delight. There were few writers of his generation who had such control over the resources of the English tongue."

In this phase of Cabellian criticism, the most denigrating critique was Peter Monro Jack's supercilious essay, "The James Branch Cabell Period," in After the Genteel Tradition, a collection of essays that Malcolm Cowley edited in 1937. Of Jurgen, Jack wrote, "There is nothing in the book that Cabell has not intimated before—but it is done here to excess, the style more flamboyant, the sexual innuendoes more salacious, the legend more romantic and correspondingly disillusioned. The censor earmarked it with uncanny precision. It is a corrupt book, as much in style as in substance, alien and insidious, and precisely what the post-war sophisticate was

James Branch Cabell   63

dreaming of." Of Cabell's work in general, he said that
"he has carried the novel of escape, pretence and sophisticated grandeur to the point of exhaustion, to the point
at which it becomes a composed philosophy of life. It is
a simple philosophy, to the effect that life is tedious,
disillusioning and scarcely worth the effort, though it
may be somewhat relieved by a dream-escape. Other
writers have made the same observation, but surely none
has had practically nothing to say and has reiterated it so
monstrously and monotonously." And of the much de-
bated Cabellian style, he wrote, "While showing every
inclination and outward sign of belonging to the small
and distinguished company of stylists, he has not, by one
notable sentence or idea, made a candid contribution of
his own. The masters with whom he has been compared,
from Petronius to Rabelais and Voltaire, made their
mark out of the life and usage of their times, not out of
cloudcuckoo land."

The only attack on Cabell that exceeds Jack's in violence is that of Oscar Cargill in his *Intellectual America:
Ideas on the March* (1941). But Cargill's attack is so
extravagant that it belongs with the literature of vituperation and not with criticism. Probably the nadir of Cabell's reputation is his being reduced to two incidental
and inconsequential references in Frederick J. Hoffman's
substantial study, *The Twenties American Writing in
the Postwar Decade* (1955).

There are, however, impressive indications of a surprising revival of interest in Cabell. Edward Wagenknecht's
judicious consideration of Cabell in his *Cavalcade of the
American Novel* (1952), Edd W. Parks's balanced reval-
uation of him in *Southern Renascence*, edited by Louis
D. Rubin, Jr. and Robert D. Jacobs (1953), and the
most penetrating and provocative of all the earlier studies, Edmund Wilson's "The James Branch Cabell Case
Reopened" (1956) may have attracted the attention of
younger critics to Cabell. At any rate, six favorable or
enthusiastic books about Cabell have appeared in the
sixties.[2]

The history of Cabell's critical reputation raises two major problems which demand attention. The first problem is that of the reasons for his lapse into almost complete obscurity for more than a decade. One of the reasons for his virtual disappearance is the abrupt changes in the socio-cultural atmosphere since the twenties, the period of his fame. The onset of the Depression in 1929 and its persistence up to the outbreak of the Second World War created an atmosphere of serious social concern to which Cabell's ironies seemed totally irrelevant. This was the decade of the social novel; this was the period when some of the best American writers flirted with the dour literary dogmas of communism. But there is an intrinsic reason for the disappearance of Cabell in periods uncongenial to his mood and tone. Of American writers who have achieved at least a brief fame, Cabell was certainly the most un-American, in even the best sense of the term. It was not merely that he was critical of phases of Americanism that other novelists satirized but that everything in his romances ran counter to the powerful movements of realism and naturalism that dominated American fiction through much of the first half of the twentieth century. Everything in his romances was alien to American literary taste: the fantastic land in which the action occurs, the drawing with utter freedom on the mythologies of many cultures, the free play of his intelligence and irony over the most cherished American beliefs and taboos. Furthermore, there were elements in Cabell's technique that alienated conventional readers. If they were looking for full-bodied three-dimensional characters and firmly built suspenseful plots, they would not find them in Cabell. Cabell's characters are not so much characters as almost allegorical expressions of a variety of attitudes toward life and philosophical positions. Even more justifiable might be annoyance with Cabell's habit of repeating situations and types of character and his regrettable habit of quoting himself again and again.

The more interesting critical problem is the question

of what, if anything, Cabell has to offer readers in a period far removed from his own. The great difficulty in judging Cabell is that he is more decidedly *sui generis* than any other American writer. In fact, the early comparisons of Cabell with Petronius and Rabelais, with Voltaire and Anatole France were not really very apt. Since Cabell is really *unique*, there is no one in comparison to whom he can be evaluated. One has to ask oneself what Cabell has to offer and whether or not one likes what he has to offer. What he has to offer is, admittedly, limited. He does not offer the substantiality and solidity of a Hemingway or the sociological subtleties of a Faulkner. Whether or not one likes what he has to offer depends on the unarguable one of the reader's personal taste. A fondness for Cabell is as unarguable as a fondness for caviar or calves's brains, the paintings of Jackson Pollock, or psychedelic posters. But it seems distinctly possible that Cabell is more relevant to the current literary atmosphere than he has been to any period since the twenties. Certainly in this period of more and more extravagant experimentation with style and form, Cabell's experiments seem distinctly modest. In a period that at its best is strenuously antirealistic and that insists on exploring the potentialities of the unconscious and the irrational, Cabell's antirealism and his wide-ranging exhibition of exotic myths and philosophies seem more relevant than they were even in the superficially sophisticated twenties. Some readers at least would find attractive one or another of the offerings in Cabell's characteristic performances: a sojourn in a fantastically imaginative Poictesme with its castles and forests, exotic flora, and enchanting landscapes, peopled by warriors, ruffians, ravishing and obliging ladies, witches, wizards, imaginary monsters, fallen gods from the great cultures, and supernatural figures that assume the forms of Pan, Satan, Janicot, Horvendile, and less sinister beings; a suave elegant and seductive style that frees itself in his later writings from his too-learned and esoteric extravagances; an incessant playful and almost disembodied eroticism; the free play of a richly cultivated mind over a wide range of views of life; a corrosive irony that undermines the seemingly dominant romanticism; a painfully, if belatedly, learned appreciation of the comforts and rewards of domesticity, and a resigned acceptance of the inevitable limitations of things-as-they-are.

John Dickson Carr

ROGER HERZEL

When at the age of fourteen I visited a private school for an admissions interview, I was already an avid reader of John Dickson Carr; and accordingly I expressed pleasure at seeing some of his novels in the small section of the school library devoted to "Books by and about Alumni." "Ah yes, John Carr '25," said the elderly master who was my guide. "I remember him well. A bright boy, but a bit of a discipline problem." He paused to laugh reminiscently. "He was a talented writer, and had literary ambitions, as I recall. But nothing ever came of it." And the conversation turned to other things.

The distinction between detective fiction and literature seemed an odd one to me at the time, but as my education progressed, I found that my guide had in fact expressed the prevailing attitude: novels are novels, and detective novels are detective novels, but detective novels are not novels. Now I find it more convenient to accept this distinction than to dispute it: in discussing Carr, whose works I continue to admire, it would be both awkward and misleading to apologize for his flat characters, his implausible plots, and his deliberate misleading of the reader; for these things, which would be serious defects in a novel considered as "literature," are both justifiable and necessary in the particular kind of fiction Carr writes.

First of all, of course, it is fiction which deals with a puzzling crime and its solution; furthermore, the reader is given all the evidence necessary to solve the crime

(Carr is scrupulous in his practice of "fair play") and is therefore in competition, tacit or stated, with the detective. But, of course, it is Carr's job to make sure that the crime is puzzling enough to hold the reader's interest, and that the reader does not solve the crime before the detective does. Thus it is necessary that the reader misunderstand the characters and their actions and inevitable that Carr should help him misunderstand by practicing some adroit misdirection. All this could be said of any "fair play" detective novelist; but it is especially applicable to Carr because of his particular devotion to the locked-room mystery.

Not all of Carr's novels fit this description; he has more than six dozen of them to his credit, and while he has established a characteristic pattern, he has also experimented with a wide variety of devices. Roughly speaking, we can divide his novels into three groups. He began his career, at the age of twenty-five, with the Inspector Bencolin mysteries; it is perhaps most fair to consider these novels a sort of apprenticeship. Then, in 1933 and 1934, he introduced his two great detectives, Dr. Gideon Fell and Sir Henry Merrivale. He continued with these two detectives, publishing the Fell novels under his own name and the Merrivale novels under the name Carter Dickson, through the end of the forties. Since that time he has become interested in mysteries set against a particular background—Napoleonic France, Restoration London, nineteenth-century New Orleans—which are historical romances as much as they are detective novels. There are exceptions to this grouping: a Dr. Fell novel still appears occasionally, and Bencolin came out of retirement to solve a crime in 1937. But the three stages of Carr's career are relatively distinct; and it is in the Fell-Merrivale novels of the thirties and forties that he made his most important contribution to the genre of the detective story.

This contribution is, once again, the locked-room mystery. Carr did not invent it, and he did not limit himself to it; but he has used it more often and more successfully than any other author. It is the heart of his first novel, *It Walks by Night* (1930).

[Bencolin] summed it up wryly: "In short, there are no secret entrances; the murderer was not hiding anywhere in the room; he did not go out by the window; he did not go out the salon door under my watching, nor the hall door under Francois'—but he was not there when we entered. Yet a murderer *had* beheaded his victim there; we know in this case above all others that the dead man did not kill himself."

The point is that there is no way the crime could have been committed. But it was. In this case, the entrances to the room were watched; in other novels, they are locked on the inside. And the range of variations on the basic principle is very wide: instead of "locked room," it is perhaps better to use the term, of which Carr himself is fond, "impossible situation." A man is found strangled in the middle of a wet clay tennis court, with only his own footsteps approaching his body. A corpse disappears from its underground vault, though the only entrance is paved over and truthful witnesses swear it has not been disturbed. In another vault, the coffins are found violently thrown about, though the smooth sand floor shows no footprint and the door is both locked and literally sealed. A man bleeds to death at the top of a ruined tower, but no living soul has come near him; it is, however, a bad neighborhood for vampires. An accused embezzler, in the presence of reliable witnesses, dives fully clothed into a small swimming pool; the clothes float to the surface, but the man has disappeared. A female archaeologist, returning home after rifling a Pharaoh's tomb, disappears from the middle of a room, leaving behind one tan mackintosh and one ancient lamp complete with curse.

Dr. Sanders, in *The Reader is Warned*, expresses well the reaction of characters faced with these situations.

Up to now, I always believed I lived in an ordered, ordinary world where nothing much ever happened. . . . In actual fact, nothing much has changed. I still eat and sleep as usual. All the wall-paper looks the same, and I don't get any more money. But I feel I've stepped over into a new kind of world where anything can happen.

The two worlds he mentions are in conflict in every one of Carr's locked-room novels. There is the common-sense, everyday world of the logically possible and the world of the seemingly miraculous which operates on different laws. The impossible situation is what suggests the existence of the second world, because it is inexplicable in terms of the first. What happened could not have happened, unless . . . And it is this "unless" that defines, in each novel, the particular second world which is suggested. Unless a murderer can melt through a solid wall, or float above wet sand and leave no footprints. Unless there are vampires or witches. Unless the hero, or his fiancée, is a murderer. In every case, supernatural or not, the second world is founded on an assumption which contradicts our experience or belief, but which is the only possible explanation for what has occurred. Or so it seems.

It is the function of the detective to destroy the miraculous world by explaining the impossible situation in terms of the practical world. Thus every novel becomes in a sense two stories, what appeared to happen and what actually did happen. The whole series of events is related twice. First the action is seen from the point of view of a character like Dr. Sanders, the observer. The reader is told only what happens in the observer's presence and what thoughts, emotions and judgments enter the observer's mind; all other characters are seen only as the observer sees them. Then, in the obligatory final chapter, the detective, speaking to the observer, recapitulates the events in the light of what he has discovered, and explains how the apparent miracle was created.

A detective who can perform such a feat must be an extraordinary man. In his earliest novels Carr seems fond of spectacularly gory murders and lurid settings, and Inspector Bencolin, as described in *The Lost Gallows*, fits right in.

The Frenchman opposite him was a tall and lazy Mephisto—Mephisto with a lifted eyebrow. His black hair was parted in the middle and twirled up like horns. Thin lines ran from his nostrils down past a small mustache and black pointed beard, past a mouth which showed now the glittering edge of a smile. His cheek-bones were high, and his eyes unfathomable. The face was brilliant, moody, capricious, and cruel. There were rings on the drooping fingers which held his cigarette. He was M. Henri Bencolin, *juge d'instruction* of the Seine, the head of the Paris police and the most dangerous man in Europe.

The description is given by Jeff Marle, the observer and narrator of most of these early novels. His function is to emphasize, with Watsonlike admiration, Bencolin's brilliance and nastiness, and also to become involved in violent and incomprehensible adventures toward the end of the novel while Bencolin is offstage, detecting. The advantage of this arrangement is obvious: Carr cannot let us watch the detective as he fits together the evidence, or the surprise of the final explanation will be gone.

After a few Bencolin novels, Carr began to experiment with less forbidding detectives. Rossiter appears only once, in *Poison in Jest*, but he is worth attention as a contrast to Bencolin.

A disreputable hat, brim turned down, was stuck on the back of his head, and from his lower lip dangled the small stump of a burnt-out cigarette. . . . He looked around with an air of refreshed and naive interest, and the most good-humoured expression I have ever seen on a human face. . . . The stranger was about my own age, with a sleepy, genial, homely face, rather fine eyes, and that perpetual air of refreshed and naive interest. He had the powerful, loose shoulders of a crew man; his slouching posture made his long arms seem even longer. His lean height was wrapped in a nondescript coat of faded and dusty green. His shoes, also nondescript, were among the largest I have ever seen; and he wore a dingy tie—with Harrow colours.

There is no need to send him offstage for his deliberations, for the workings of his mind are concealed from the reader both because the narrator considers him a lunatic and pays little attention to him and because his utterances are so incoherent that they make no sense except in retrospect, when he finally gives a lucid reconstruction of the crime.

Poison in Jest marks a turning point in Carr's career, away from Bencolin and toward Dr. Gideon Fell and Sir Henry Merrivale. The two have much in common. Like Bencolin, they are universally respected as geniuses in the art of solving mysteries, but neither has any official connection with the police; each works only as an informal adviser to a Scotland Yard man—Merrivale to Chief Inspector Masters, Fell to Chief Inspector (later Superintendent) Hadley.

Both detectives share an eccentric amiability with their predecessor Rossiter. It seems that Carr has abandoned his all-out effort to shock the reader with the combination of an impossible situation, a ghastly crime, and an inhuman detective, and has begun instead to build on the contrast between sinister and baffling crime and the comfortable common sense which puts these forces of darkness to rout. Rossiter, Fell, and Merrivale are more appropriate representatives of this common sense because they are more believable—not because they are necessarily any less farfetched than Bencolin, but simply because it is more pleasant and therefore easier to believe in them.

Sir Henry Merrivale never smiles. He scowls, sneers, leers, and snarls, and his most frequent expression is one of "almost inhuman malignancy"; but this ill-temper is assumed partly in a futile effort to achieve dignity, partly in protest at everyone's failure to take him seriously. We are told that he "once managed all the sleight-of-hand known as the British Military Intelligence Department," and we are given this description of him, in *The White Priory Murders*, by his American brother-in-law:

Don't, under any circumstances, use any ceremony with him. He wouldn't understand it. He has frequently got into trouble at political meetings by making speeches in which he absent-mindedly refers to their Home Secretary as Boko and their Premier as Horse-face. You will probably find him asleep, although he will pretend he is very busy. His favorite delusion is that he is being persecuted, and that nobody appreciates him. His baronetcy is two or three hundred years old, and he is also a fighting Socialist. He is a qualified barrister and physician, and he speaks the world's most slovenly grammar. His mind is scurrilous; he shocks lady typists, wears white socks, and appears in public without his necktie. Don't be deceived by his looks; he likes to think he is as expressionless as a Buddha and as sour-faced as Scrooge. I may add . . . that at criminal investigation he is a good deal of a genius.

Dr. Fell is less comic and more genial. We are given less information about his background, but he appears to be a retired professor whose field is esoteric information; in different novels he proves an expert on Satanism, witchcraft, the history of Transylvania, and fortune-telling, among other things. He is enormously fat, red-faced and untidy, walks with the help of two canes, and reminds those who meet him of Old King Cole.

Merrivale and Fell form an interesting contrast to Bencolin in terms of their mental abilities. At first, Carr apparently thought that the quality most useful in solving puzzles was pure intelligence, and that intelligence excluded feeling; the cold reasoner was what was needed, and the coldness implied a streak of cruelty. Both Merrivale and Fell, on the other hand, are described as childlike; and their mystery-solving ability lies not so much in pure reason as in their habit of seeing all things, large and small, as of equal significance. For example, in *The Three Coffins* the victim buys a large painting, seven feet by four, has it wrapped in brown paper, and easily carries it away unaided. Later in the day the painting, still wrapped, is delivered to the victim's house by two burly men who have great difficulty in getting it upstairs. These two facts are given to the reader surrounded by material of much greater apparent significance; and neither the reader, nor any character in the novel, notices the discrepancy, except for Dr. Fell. He is the only one who notices that the picture has gained weight on the way home; he wonders what large, flat, rectangular object that might be hidden in the package could be so damnably heavy; he realizes that the presence of that object in the victim's room could explain how the apparent murderer apparently disappeared, and the mystery is a long way toward being solved.

Carr has been fair with us. He has given us all the information he gave Dr. Fell. We could have solved that mystery (or so we like to believe) if only we had noticed that little discrepancy about the weight of the package. But we did not notice it, because we did not realize it could be important. Fell's advantage over us is that he never realizes anything can be unimportant; everything is equally and indiscriminately interesting to him. Examples could be multiplied for Fell and Merrivale alike. Lady Helen Loring is not photogenic. A lesser maidservant has been given the day off. These two trivial facts, taken together, explain the mysterious disappearance of Lady Helen in *The Curse of the Bronze Lamp*. But only Merrivale would think to put these two facts together, or even to notice them. The reader knew them as soon as Merrivale did; but his interest was so occupied with the seemingly more important matter of a Pharaoh's curse—in *The Three Coffins* it was Transylvanian ghouls—that he never stopped to think about the facts. Carr does mislead us, but he is fair about it.

The detective's interest in such trivia is a constant source of exasperation to the professional policeman, Masters or Hadley. Besides serving as a character-foil to the detective—methodical persistence against imaginative brilliance—he serves the purpose of validating the miracle, that is, for example, assuring the detective and the reader that the locked room is really locked and contains no secret passages or other such inartistic cheats. He also supplies the detective with routine technical information—criminal records, chemical analyses, fingerprints, and so on. Most important of all, the personal friendship and rivalry existing between the two men frequently takes the form of a battle of wits in which the detective directs the policeman's attention to certain important pieces of evidence and challenges him (and, of course, the reader) to see their significance.

The observer is the third person involved in solving the mystery. He is Carr's link with the reader, and his main function is to present the reader with an accurate picture of the facts themselves and an inaccurate picture of their importance. He is generally a physician or a lawyer; the reader will thus automatically assume his reliability as a witness, giving him, or rather his profession, credit for the ability to handle evidence accurately and objectively. And every clue is given, as we have seen; to this extent the reader's faith is justified.

But the observer is also very frequently young, and likely to react emotionally to the other characters. He can thus in perfect honesty mislead the reader as to the interpretation of the evidence because of his failure to sympathize with one character, or because of his excessive sympathy for another.

His mistaken reactions to the other characters are useful in another way. Carr cannot give a full characterization of a murderer while concealing both the fact that he has committed murder and the emotions that led him to do it. But he can paint a vivid and convincing, though inaccurate, portrait of him as seen by the observer. These temporary characterizations tend to be quite good; it is only when the truth is known that the characters look like puppets, and at that point of the novel it scarcely matters.

The observer tends to become directly involved in the action, often at considerable risk to his own safety. This perhaps needs no justification: suspense and adventure are good in themselves, and it would not fit the Olympian image of Fell or Merrivale to be in danger. It may be pointed out, however, that as long as the reader is thinking about dangerous adventures he is not thinking about solutions to the locked-room puzzle.

It is perhaps for this reason that Carr so often sets the detective, policeman and observer, who theoretically are working together, at cross purposes. In *The Problem of the Wire Cage*, for example, the observer finds evidence which indicates that his fiancée has committed the murder. He wants to conceal the evidence, the detective wants to find out the truth, and the policeman, who has his job to think of, wants to make an arrest. On the other hand, in *She Died a Lady*, the observer—an old doctor this time—works furiously to solve the murder of a friend, and does rather well in spite of Merrivale's curious uncooperativeness. It turns out that Merrivale was deliberately obstructing the doctor's efforts so that he would not discover that the murderer was his son. In other novels, the detective arrives at the solution but is unable to present enough proof to win a conviction; he must therefore lay a trap for the murderer, misleading the policeman and the observer (and, incidentally, the reader) about his true intentions so that the murderer will not suspect the trap.

With all these complications it is easy for the reader to lose sight of what is supposedly his main concern: the race with the detective to solve the puzzle.

It is worth noting that this group of three allies, which is useful to Carr in so many ways, exists only in the Fell-Merrivale novels, not in the Bencolin novels or the historical romances; and the locked-room device is less developed in these earlier and later novels. Carr was able to combine the impossible situation and the fair-play method most effectively when he separated the detective from the policeman; thus the transition from Bencolin to Fell and Merrivale marks an advance in technique. The second transition, to historical romances, indicates only that Carr has become interested in a different kind of fiction, in which the detective plot is of secondary importance. But even here it is possible to see vestiges of the conflict between the three allies, though detective, policeman, and observer have now been combined into one character. In most of the romances, for example, the duels and love affairs of the hero interfere with his detective work; or to choose a more elaborate example, in *The Devil in Velvet* Nicholas Fenton, a middle-aged, twentieth-century history professor, sells his soul to the devil for the privilege of inhabiting the body of his Restoration namesake; he wants to prevent a murder. As a result, one character is literally two men: he retains the "mind, knowledge, memory and experience" of Professor Fenton, in uneasy combination with the youthful passion and fatal lack of self-control of Sir Nicholas.

Since in these romances the detective's view of the action is the same as the reader's, competition between detective and reader is scarcely possible. The Fell-Merrivale novels are more appropriately designed as a test of the reader's wits, and it is traditional to assume that this is why one reads a detective story.

But perhaps even in the Fell-Merrivale novels this traditional assumption is misleading; perhaps it is more profitable to think of reader and author as accomplices rather than adversaries. The audience goes to see the magician not for confirmation of its belief in the more obvious laws of nature but for evidence of their apparent suspension. In *The Gilded Man* Merrivale gives a skillful amateur conjuring performance to a group of parish children. Their chaperone, a Miss Clutterbuck, persists in giving an audible and accurate explanation of each trick as Merrivale performs it. She is rewarded by being gagged, bound to a chair, and dropped through a trap door. No one would question the appropriateness of her punishment: the children came to be mystified, not instructed, and any audience seeking entertainment has a stake in the success of the performer. The mystery story is by convention a battle of wits; but it is also, by convention, a battle which the reader will lose; it remains interesting to the last chapter as long as the reader is one step behind, not ahead of, the detective. Very few readers really want to lose interest in a story halfway through; most will take good care to remain baffled.

The analogy between Carr's impossible situations and the tricks of a stage magician is a tempting one, made more so by the frequent appearance in the novels of professional magicians, as victims or suspects or advisers to the detective. The devices themselves are similar both in the mechanics of their operation and in their dependence on misdirection, which the magician accomplishes by sleight of hand and Carr by manipulation, through the observer, of point of view. Both tend to depend frequently on "atmosphere" to put the audience in the proper frame of mind: the magician uses exotic or supernatural hocus-pocus in exactly the same way that Carr uses haunted houses, abandoned castles, sinister foreigners, and cults of Satan-worshippers. The analogy, however, breaks down, as analogies have a way of doing, when we come to the detective; for there is no equivalent for him in the situation of the stage-magician—except for Miss Clutterbuck and such spoilsports. She is an intruder in the performance because she disrupts the proper relationship between the performer and his audience by doing precisely what the detective does: reminding the audience of the practical world just when it is in the mood to believe in the magical world. She and the magician are working at cross purposes.

It is not quite correct to say that Carr and his detectives are working at cross purposes, since the detective's work is obviously part of Carr's purpose. But it is proper to say that Carr is trying to do two conflicting things, that he is building with one hand and destroying with the other. And it is perhaps natural that there should be some disappointment once the detective has solved the crime and revealed the miracle to be nothing but a combination of more or less clever planning and perverse chance, or what Merrivale calls "the blinkin' awful cussedness of things in general." The problem is discussed at some length in *The Three Coffins*; the first speaker is O'Rourke, a vaudeville performer, talking about stage-illusions, and the second is Dr. Fell himself, talking about detective stories.

It's a funny thing about people. They go to see an illusion; you tell 'em it's an illusion; they pay their money to see an illusion. And yet for some funny reason they get sore because it isn't *real* magic. When they hear an explanation of how somebody got out of a locked box or a roped sack that they've examined, they get sore because it *was* a trick. They say it's farfetched when they know how they were deceived. Now, it takes BRAINS, I'm telling you, to work out one of those simple tricks. . . . But they never think of the cleverness it takes just to fool 'em under their noses. I think they'd like the secret of an escape to be some unholy business like real magic; something that nobody on God's earth could ever do.

. . . .

Now, it seems reasonable to point out that the word improbable is the very last which should ever be used to curse detective fiction in any case. A great part of our liking for detective fiction is *based* on a liking for improbability. When A is murdered, and B and C are under strong suspicion, it is improbable that the innocent-looking D can be guilty. But he is. . . . In short, you come to a point where the word improbable grows meaningless as a jeer. There can be no such thing as any probability until the end of the story. And then, if you wish the murder to be fastened on an unlikely person (as some of us old fogies do), you can hardly complain because he acted from motives less likely or necessarily less apparent than those of the person first suspected. . . .

Why are we dubious when we hear the explanation of the locked room? Not in the least because we are incredulous, but simply because in some vague way we are *disappointed*. And from that feeling it is only natural to take an unfair step farther, and call the whole business incredible or impossible or flatly ridiculous.

Precisely, in short, . . . what O'Rourke was telling us today about illusions that are performed *in real life*. . . . And the secret of both disappointments in the same—we expect too much.

You see, the effect is so magical that we somehow expect the cause to be magical also. When we see that it isn't wizardry, we call it tomfoolery. Which is hardly fair play.

If Dr. Fell is right, then *The Burning Court* should be Carr's most satisfactory novel. Gaudan Cross is the detective here. He is a connoisseur of crime, and writes highly successful biographies of the great murderers. He is also a murderer himself, having planned and executed an undetectable murder to prove that it could be done; however, he made the mistake of bragging about it, and as a result served a long prison sentence, during which he acquired much practical information about crime from his fellow experts. The mystery he is called upon to solve is the best vintage Carr: a case of poison, administered by a woman in old-fashioned costume entering the victim's room through a door which had been bricked up in 1707. There is also a disappearing corpse and a good deal of superstition, neatly divided between the Pennsylvania Dutch servants and the stolid young hero's pretty wife, whose French-Canadian foster mother raised her in the firm belief that she was a witch. In the obligatory final scene, Cross dispels the superstitions, explains the miracles, and confronts the murderer; he then proposes a toast, raises his glass of sherry, drinks, and dies at once of cyanide poisoning, thus casting grave doubts upon his infallibility. In an epilogue, we learn that the pretty young wife is a witch after all.

And so, for once, the sinister forces of the unknown triumph over the force of reason which tried to explain them away. It is the sort of ending that Carr can only use once—it undermines the basic premise of his fiction, and is a waste of a good detective—but it is also the sort of ending that his novels seem to demand, and it is satisfying to see him assert for once that the magician's tricks are in fact magic and not tricks. We scarcely need Dr. Fell to point out the extent to which probability has been sacrificed; but anyone with a passion for the probable is not the sort of reader who is likely to be attracted to the novels of John Dickson Carr.

Nathanael West
The Use of Cynicism

BRUCE OLSEN

In a small way Nathanael West lived and wrote himself
into the myths that America conjured up about itself in
the twenties and thirties. Among the uses of the word
myth is that which means a commonly accepted but
stereotyped social pattern, such as the Horatio Alger
myth; and in each of his four short novels, West bom-
barded, sometimes in the manner of a soured infant, not
only Horatio Alger but also grassroots democracy, Christian compassion, and Hollywood's dream of America.
West would have us stand implacably undeceived
against the storymakers. Life, as he seemed to proclaim
it, did blindly run with unconscious desires, uncharted
social forces, and the indifferent blows of accident. Myth
was what man used to get on with it until that too was
stripped from him. He is almost never guilty of giving us
hope or a positive feeling. Nihilism, I suppose, is the
closest word, though I am about to suggest that his work
succeeds only when he found a formal, intrinsic way of
displacing it.

By a wide critical consensus West is a one-and-a-half-
book writer, the one being a perfectly shaped little masterpiece, *Miss Lonelyhearts* (1933), and the half a savage, promising, and unfulfilled novel about Hollywood,
The Day of the Locust (1939). My argument centers on
a problem of evaluation. On the one hand, West is
valued as an emblem of an era of violent exploration:
"Fitzgerald saw the mockery," says James F. Light,

"Deep in his bones, Nathanael West felt it. He had written about nothing else." [1] West himself lived as if to touch every image of protest. He was, in succession, a dandified Flaming Youth in college, a Parisian expatriate, a fellow traveler, a Jew who changed his name in order to "Go West" (his own pun), a Hollywood screenwriter who agonized over his loss of purity while collecting three hundred and fifty dollars a week. He existed on a minor stage of publicity, having the acquaintance of many famous writers; S. J. Perelman was his brother-in-law, and Eileen McKenney, the prototype for *My Sister Eileen*, became his wife shortly before his death. And finally, he lived out the role of the idealistic and ignored serious writer, capable of such standard film inspiration as *Five Came Back*, and was cut down at the age of thirty-seven in that archetype of American futile endings, the automobile accident. Everything about West suggested the role-player, the wearer of masks, though none of them definitively. In his injured idealism there is more than a breath of the old romantic agony. He lived and wrote as the uncompromising compromised man who symbolized something in our history that we need to digest.

On the other hand, we have the texts of his four novels, which another generation needs to evaluate on its own. Since 1957 they have been available in one squat volume which sits a little too lightly in the hand; we have here no Byron, no Thomas Wolfe, but a slender collection too often precious in manner and over explicit in assertion. Without the fine quality of *Miss Lonelyhearts* we should not find enough stature in West's writing to make him the representative figure he has become. And, my argument continues, *Miss Lonelyhearts* succeeds not because its pessimistic anger is greater than that of the others but for old-fashioned formal reasons. That novel (or perhaps it should be called a novella) gives us the only instance in which West succeeded in using his views instead of declaring them. His writing provides a good test case for exploring intrinsic and extrinsic value, the difference between the operation of a work and the social-literary emblem.

What makes *Miss Lonelyhearts* superior to *A Cool Million* (1934)? The latter is generally agreed to be a failure, "formless, an inorganic stringing together of comic set-pieces, with the preposterous incidents serving merely to raise the various topics West chooses to satirize," according to Stanley Edgar Hyman.[2] Subtitled "The Dismantling of Lemuel Pitkin," it is an attempt to create an American Candide legitimized by the style and melodramatic maneuvering of Horatio Alger. As a social document it is remarkable for its early recognition of fascism and its mid-depression ridicule of the American Dream; clearly, there are many extrinsic reasons for praising it: "In its awareness of political technique, its devastatingly true analysis of unrestricted Capitalist method, its foreshadowing of Americanism turned into a possible Fascism, *A Cool Million* is brilliantly successful," says Alan Ross before charging it with stylistic inadequacy.[3]

West's satire quickly finds its objects and dogs them relentlessly. Young Lemuel Pitkin and his sweetheart, Betty Prail, pass from episode to episode, he losing an eye, his hair, his teeth, and a leg to the greed and malice of those he trusts, while she passes from hand to hand among the white slavers. West carefully imitates Alger's formula of coincidental encounter and melodramatic heroism with, however, the ironic twist of the hero receiving a vicious kick instead of a just reward. Having rescued a young girl from being trampled to death by horses and having lost an eye in the process, for example, Lemuel is tricked into signing a waiver by the father of the girl (who also owns the horses) releasing him from any damages. The single, monotonous, and brittle tone of the whole work can, I think, be fairly represented in short quotations. Captured by Indians, Lemuel, Betty, and their Indian friend, Jake Raven, are led to a village.

The chief's name was Israel Satinpenny. He had been to Harvard and hated the white man with undying venom. For many years now, he had been trying to get the Indian nations to rise and drive the palefaces back to the countries from which they had come, but so far he had had little success. His people had grown soft and lost their warlike ways. Perhaps, with the wanton wounding of Jake Raven, his chance had come.[4]

In the chief's harangue to his tribe we get such labored wit as "The star of the paleface is sinking and he knows it. Spengler has said so; Valéry has said so; thousands of his wise men proclaim it."[5] This shrill consistency is maintained throughout; it is an opinion, or a bundle of opinions, not too difficult to agree with but conceived by and held in the authority of the narrator alone. The narrator holds all the cards. No one of the characters is sufficiently developed as a center of intelligence and feeling to be other than an instrument of the narrator's devices.

We have, in other words, a book praiseworthy by most extrinsic standards—for its political acumen, its representation of its time, its justified philosophical anger, perhaps even for its attempt of literary assimilation. Yet history's literary judgment has surely proclaimed it a failure. Why is it not the representative book of a representative author?

My answer is a general one which goes beyond the problem of West's writing. To succeed firmly a novel must be a process created and extended by a dual control of the actual behavior of language. What we have presented to us is not "life" or a system of ideas and feelings, but, most properly, a double contention revealed in the authority in which the book is expressed. A Cool Million is univocal; Miss Lonelyhearts is not. No amount of attitude, no matter how timely or perceptive, will give us a process formed by an internally operating conflict. The conflict of A Cool Million, such as it is, is only that between a platitude and a sneer, a contest so quickly over that we can find no excitement in it.

Miss Lonelyhearts, in contrast, is a marvelous example of emotions deferred in internal structure. It is the story of a lovelorn columnist with a "Christ complex," torn between his compassion for the miserable people who write to him, his own desire for a happy life, and the vicious cynicism of his feature editor, Shrike. He eventually becomes involved with a cripple and his frustrated wife and dies with as firm a tragic inevitability as modern literature has produced.

This time the control of the language is shared between the narrator and Miss Lonelyhearts—a distinction which I feel is much more than a technical one because it allows the feelings of both to be expressed in the flow of language, and in point-to-point conflict.

He entered the park at the North Gate and swallowed mouthfuls of the heavy shade that curtained its arch. He walked into the shadow of a lamp-post that lay on the path like a spear. It pierced him like a spear.

As far as he could discover, there were no signs of spring. The decay that covered the surface of the mottled ground was not the kind in which life generates. Last year, he remembered, May had failed to quicken these soiled fields. It had taken all the brutality of July to torture a few green spikes through the exhausted dirt.[6]

There is nothing unusual about this passage in which the imagery is in part derived from Eliot's *The Waste Land,* but the participation of both the narrator and the point of view is clearly visible, as it is throughout. This cross-fertilization of language is a technique as old as Henry James, James Joyce, and other modern masters; nothing new, but West had caught up with it. The narrator is evident in the tight, rather self-conscious prose rhythms ("May had failed to quicken the soiled fields"), the assonance, consonance, and alliteration ("the shadow of a lamp-post that lay on the path like a spear"), and the metaphorical and syntactical control generally. On the other hand, the images, the setting, and the pattern of thought follow the despair and confused ruminations of Miss Lonelyhearts. Both the narrator and Miss Lonelyhearts are dramatized by the activity of language itself, so that they are felt as at least partial personalities. The narrator is removed, objective, controlled, analytical of feelings, and quite aware of the unfeeling backdrop against which passion is played out. Miss Lonelyhearts is despairing, lonely, confused by both pity and cruelty, impulsive, subjective, and uncontrolled.

The narrator nevertheless retains the overview, the power of selection, the determinant of what goes into this particular fictive universe and what stays out. It has the ultimate responsibility for the grounds of the fiction and a strategy for producing the effect of inevitability. One important matter that stays in is the brilliant cynicism of Shrike, Miss Lonelyhearts' intelligent and sadistic boss.

My friend, I know of course that neither the soil, nor the South Seas, nor hedonism, nor suicide, nor drugs, can mean anything to us. We are not men who swallow camels only to strain at stools. God alone is our escape. The church is our only hope, the First Church of Christ Dentist, where He is worshiped as Preventer of Decay. The church whose symbol is the trinity new-style: Father, Son, and Wirehaired Fox Terrier . . . And so, my good friend, let me dictate a letter to Christ for you.[7]

The illusion of inevitable disaster in a despairing world is contrived under the authority of the narrator by limiting the possible alternatives. The suffering of those who write to Miss Lonelyhearts is real and probable; we know that there are such people, and undoubtedly an advice columnist would receive such mail. Broken, ignorant, psychologically and physically crippled, they are indeed betrayed by their desires. Most of us can evade such a mass of pity; the strategy of the book is to make it appear omnipresent and inescapable.

Dear Miss Lonelyhearts —
I am writing to you for my little sister Gracie because something awfull hapened to her and I am afraid to tell mother about it. I am 15 years old and Gracie is 13 and we live in Brooklyn. Gracie is deaf and dumb and biger than me but not very smart on account of being deaf and dumb. . . . Last week a man came on the roof and did something dirty to her. . . . If I tell mother she will beat Gracie up awfull

because I am the only one who loves her and last time when she tore her dress they loked her in the closet for 2 days and if the boys on the blok hear about it they will say dirty things like they did on Peewee Conors sister the time she got caught in the lots.[8]

The series of letters, piercing, utterly pathetic, and yet genuine, constitute the images of horror which Miss Lonelyhearts must either deal with or escape. To every possible answer Shrike is ready with his devastating cynicism; and, indeed, if humanity is as limited as these letter writers, there is little hope.

The principal figure of hope for Miss Lonelyhearts is his girl friend, Betty, who returns his love. Why not happiness if they are both in love? Why should he not evade the horror of the world with the same power of repression and positive relationships which most are able to find? The possibility of romance is only raised to close it off as an avenue of escape. The inadequacy of this solution is foreshadowed in a variety of ways. Betty, for instance, believes that a trip into the country will cure his depression—a shallow view in respect to his morbid condition. But this prospect has already been undermined by Shrike's catalogue of impossible escapes; and although the brief time he spends in Connecticut with Betty is happy, the only upbeat episode in the story, he is soon beset with more letters and new problems upon his return. Furthermore, two other sexual encounters, one with Mrs. Shrike, the other with Mrs. Doyle, the cripple's wife, indicate to him that the anguished world somehow has a claim upon his body as well as upon his soul. Betty becomes pregnant; they agree to marry, but Miss Lonelyhearts is shot down by the jealous Doyle just as he approaches him in the delusion that he can cure his affliction with Christlike powers.

The narrator presides over this grinding view of fate and makes it seem possible. The Christian view of grace, so longingly sought for by Miss Lonelyhearts, is "proved" inadequate in this fictional real. Yet the pessimism is such that few would accept it as a philosophical proposition—the widespread activity of the race shows that it can't be all *that* bad—and certainly as statement it would neither provoke nor convince. In short, *Miss Lonelyhearts* is effective because for once West found a strategy for ordering attitudes within the work and thus cast the reality in which the story was possible. The attack upon Christian compassion as a delusive myth is made to work by enforcing a quite contrary mythlike view—that the universe is composed of deterministic forces in which feeling has no relevance.

The Day of the Locust dallies with sensational material and fails to deliver its full impact for reasons which, once more, are formal. Hollywood's fantastic dream factory of the thirties of course existed; it made myths and inspired its citizens to live as if these myths were real; and by this fact challenged the artistic imagination to catch up to the social reality. Whatever the reality may have been, the novel is crowded with such matter as cock fights, malicious child stars, perverts, and grotesques, and ends in a mindless orgiastic riot. ("I adore smut," one matron says at a party; the gimmick of the evening is an artificial dead horse in the swimming pool.) [9] From beginning to end it is a wild (and yet quite moralistic) assault on the senses. It is a conscious depiction of the moral desert, Hollywood style, which Svidrigailov knew and prophesied for Raskolnikov. Given its energy and firsthand authority, it should be better than it is.

The burden of the point of view falls mainly to Tod Hackett, an artist who has "sold out" to Hollywood but who nevertheless retains enough idealistic impulse to paint a large canvas, "The Burning of Los Angeles," in which he incorporates his experiences into art. In a middle section the point of view is given over to Homer Simpson, an awkward oaf from the Middle West who somehow manages to preserve his innocence as the insanity tumbles about him. This shift is a major structural mistake, and Homer is allowed to drift off at the end, determined to return home. The link between the two is their mutual attraction for Faye Greener, beautiful, ambitious, and untalented, who belongs to the unsuccessful hangers-on of Hollywood, and who induces most of the story's action through her escapades.

The writing is again dominated by an over-explicit narrator. Tod, and especially Homer, are too passive to learn significantly. They do not share in controlling the language in a fundamental way; they drift from episode to episode, reacting, but not demonstrating any important shift in sensibility. Homer, for instance, is seen as a gawking fool who has no control over his hands:

> Homer spent the rest of the afternoon in the broken deck chair. The lizard was on the cactus, but he took little interest in its hunting. His hands kept his thoughts busy. They trembled and jerked, as though troubled by dreams. To hold them still, he clasped them together. Their fingers twined like a tangle of thighs in miniature. He snatched them apart and sat on them.[10]

It is clear that Homer cannot express or even realize the unconscious forces pushing him, and therefore cannot begin to enter the frame of reference so intelligently developed by the narrator. He remains something only seen and acted upon. But Tod, though intelligent and articulate, does not fare much better as a carrier of the drama. He is never more than mildly seduced by the frenetic activity around him, and has no powerful motives toward or against anything or anyone. Indeed he learns that Hollywood is a monstrous place, but this requires little perspicacity in view of the narrator's treatment. His personal resolution is supposed to come about in his artistic vision, "The Burning of Los Angeles." Yet this aspect of the man is so sketchily treated, so undramatized in language and generally unconvincing, that it does not move the story to fulfillment.

> As he stood on his good leg, clinging desperately to the iron rail, he could see all the rough charcoal strokes with which he had blocked it out on the big canvas. Across the top, parallel with the frame, he had drawn the burning city, a great bonfire of architectural styles, ranging from Egyptian to Cape Cod colonial. Through the center, winding from left

to right, was a long hill street and down it, spilling into the middle foreground, came the mob carrying baseball bats and torches. For the faces of its members, he was using the innumerable sketches he had made of the people who come to California to die; the cultists of all sorts, economic as well as religious, the wave, airplane, funeral and preview watchers —all those poor devils who can only be stirred by the promise of miracles and then only to violence.[11]

This is considerably less of a vision—a mere verbal reduction, in fact—of the grim texture of the whole. Tod amounts to little more than a faceless alter ego of the narrator, an observant lens to move about from scene to scene, and with no emotions except those more significantly declared by the narrator. And no matter how intelligent and forceful the narrator may be, he needs language-demonstrated moral learning in some other center than himself for an adequate conflict and resolution. In the middle of the riot Tod is given a page of straight interior monologue which sums up his moral conclusions:

All their lives they had slaved at some kind of dull, heavy labor, behind desks and counters, in the fields and at tedious machines of all sorts, saving their pennies and dreaming of the leisure that would be theirs when they had enough. Finally that day came. . . . Where else should they go but California, the land of sunshine and oranges?

Once there, they discover that sunshine isn't enough. They get tired of oranges, even of avocado pears and passion fruit. Nothing happens. . . . What else is there? They watch the waves come in at Venice. There wasn't any ocean where most of them came from, but after you've seen one wave, you've seen them all. . . . If only a plane would crash once in a while so that they could watch the passengers being consumed in a "holocaust of flame," as the newspapers put it.[12]

A good description of boredom, we may say, and no doubt sociologically accurate and just. But is this what Tod Hackett has learned? Hasn't the narrator long since been indicating this emptiness and boredom, and hasn't the sympathetic reader been following? It is simply too explicit. *The Day of the Locust* fails, as do many novels, in the confusion between moral earnestness and effective structure. Compare Tod's reaction, for instance, to the fine and paradoxical moment of another cynic under similar circumstances, Nick Carraway, who for the first time perceives what Gatsby is really like: " 'They're a rotten crowd,' I shouted across the lawn. 'You're worth the whole damn bunch put together.' I've always been glad I said that." Homer Simpson, who might have served a function similar to that of Gatsby, clearly does not because of the inadequate creation of Tod's character.

Myths and the mythmakers are taken up and exploited, but myth itself is not established. With all its savagery and indignation as a starting point, *The Day of the Locust* should have been what the dust jacket proclaims, "the best novel ever written about Hollywood."

The Dream Life of Balso Snell (1931), the first of West's novels, is the best to consider last. An esoteric early effort, apparently started when he was at college and finished as he worked as the assistant manager of two Manhattan hotels, its publishing history (five hundred privately printed copies quickly forgotten) is perfectly consonant with its experimental, Parisian nature. It is at once trivial and serious, silly and funny, crude and sophisticated—all the signs of immaturity with great promise. And what it shows about West as a writer is quite to our point.

Balso Snell is a dream fantasy, and as such employs a representation of the primary process in which causality, time sequence, space, and the coherence of images are deliberately distorted; no ego-dominated concept of "structure" could be relevant to its mode. Balso Snell, a poet, enters the Trojan Horse through the anus and meets a variety of figures, some of whom change shape during the encounter, who deliver interpolated stories and manuscripts, and sometimes interpolations within interpolations, making the story line complex indeed. There is, for instance, Maloney the Areopagite who tells the story of Saint Puce, a flea who dwelt in the armpit of Christ, "drinking His blood"; a "Crime Journal" of John Raskolnikov Gilson, found in a tree, and which turns out to be written by a sexually precocious schoolboy in short pants; a nymph who evanesces into Miss McGeeney, a middle-aged schoolteacher, and so on. Episodes pass on unevenly and without dramatic formulation until it ends with Balso's wet dream. The whole is characterized by a scatological fury, a toilet image of disgust for every conceivable human aspiration or institution, "Written while smelling the moistened forefinger of my left hand." [13] Light has pointed out the direct inspiration of surrealism, Dadaism, and the *Walpurgisnacht* section of Joyce's *Ulysses*.[14]

Its anarchic moral absolutism would be difficult to overstate; desire of every kind is a delusion and corruption. Balso, viewing the girls in the lobby of Carnegie Hall, "likened their disarranged hips, their short legs, their humps, their splay feet, their wall-eyes, to ornament." It is a typical rather than an emphatic passage.[15] The argument against the vanity of the will is hardly less severe than that of the ancient Cynic, Antisthenes, who is supposed to have said, "I had rather go mad than experience pleasure." Thus Beagle Darwin, who is relieved when his pregnant mistress commits suicide, is represented as a sentimental fool for having any feelings at all. The schoolboy, in a pamphlet which he hands to Balso describing his love affair with Saniette, gives one of the best statements about the conflict between will and desire:

"When you think of me, Saniette," I said, "think of two men—myself and the chauffeur within me. This chauffeur is very large and dressed in ugly ready-made clothing. His shoes, soiled from walking about the streets of a great city, are covered with animal ordure and chewing gum. His hands are covered with coarse woollen gloves. On his head is a derby hat."

"The name of this chauffeur is The Desire to Procreate."

"He sits within me like a man in an automobile. His heels are in my bowels, his knees on my heart, his face in my brain. His gloved hands hold me firmly by the tongue; his hands, covered with wool, refuse me speech for the emotions aroused by the face in my brain." [16]

West reserves a special emphasis, however, for the vanity of art. Time after time we are told that artistic pretension is absurd, that the quest for beauty is a snare. The incorporated parody of *Crime and Punishment* seems to show that even Dostoyevsky, the novelist that West most admired, could and should be reduced to jiggling irrelevance. The purity of resignation! It is better never to have sought an ideal of art than to have one disappointed; or, as Beagle Darwin maintains, "the only place to commit suicide is on Chekov's grave." [17] If art is foolish desire, then foolish desire is no more than the automaton of sex, according to the rampant associations which reinforce one another; Miss McGeeney reports the views of the biographer Perkins who "had found in the odors of a woman's body, never-ending, ever-fresh variation and change—a world of dreams, seas, roads, forests, textures, colors, flavors, forms. . . . He told me that he had built from the odors of his wife's body an architecture and an aesthetic, a music and a mathematic." [18] We arrive ultimately at the anarchist gesture of Dadaism. "In case the audience should misunderstand and align itself on the side of the artist," the schoolboy says in his pamphlet, "the ceiling of the theatre will be made to open and cover the occupants with tons of loose excrement. After the deluge, if they so desire, the patrons of my art can gather in the customary charming groups and discuss the play." [19]

Yet *Balso Snell* exists in the paradox between the assertion of a negative absolute and its own careful performance. It is not, after all, a Dadaist performance, but an intense execution of the art of anti-art. Its morbid thrust was soon to be displaced into the character of Shrike, who in turn is displaced into a structure whose conception is in itself the strongest possible affirmation of art. When Shrike flails at Miss Lonelyhearts, that cynicism is multiplied by the mirrors of a powerful artistic conception. And it is that system of mirrors, I should suppose, and not the emblems or the philosophy, which gives us the candlepower for a myth.

West was too close to a philosophy of value to achieve objectivity. But he did achieve it once, and he came reasonably close another time, which is more than most of us do, and is worth remembering.

Flannery O'Connor
The Soul of the Grotesque

PAUL LEVINE

"Ordinary life has a grotesque dimension," observes a character in Saul Bellow's "The Wen," "and this has become a theme of the times." Perhaps the first writer to treat the grotesque as a manifestation of everyday experience was Sherwood Anderson. In *Winesburg, Ohio* Anderson not only took for his metaphor the word which has come to stand for a whole genre of American writing, but he prefaced his stories with a manifesto entitled "The Book of the Grotesque." In it he expounded his theory of the grotesque:

That in the beginning when the world was young there were a great many thoughts but no such thing as truth. Man made the truths himself and each truth was a composite of a great many vague thoughts. All about in the world were the truths and they were all beautiful.

The old man had listed hundreds of the truths in his book. I will not try to tell you all of them. There was the truth of virginity and the truth of passion, the truth of wealth and of poverty, of thrift and of profligacy, of carelessness and abandon. Hundreds and hundreds were the truths and they were all beautiful.

And then the people came along. Each as he appeared snatched up one of the truths and some who were quite strong snatched up a dozen of them.

It was the truths that made the people grotesques. The old man had quite an elaborate theory concerning the matter. It was his notion that the moment one of the people took one of the truths to himself, called it his truth, and tried to live his life by it, he became a grotesque and the truth he embraced became a falsehood.

Winesburg, Ohio is about the truths that people in this small town squeeze into falsehoods by trying to live their lives by them. But Anderson's vision in these stories is double. On the one hand, he describes the social fabric of the town in which a stern Puritan morality represses the natural expression of emotions. On the other hand, he reveals the private worlds of these unhappy people whose secret dreams are frustrated by their inability to communicate. But throughout, Anderson is clearly sympathetic with his grotesques whose stories are "delicious, like the twisted little apples that grow in the orchards of Winesburg." In reacting to their beauty he is like Doctor Reefy's wife who, once she "had discovered the sweetness of the twisted apples . . . could not get her mind fixed again upon the round perfect fruit that is eaten in the city apartments."

To a younger generation of readers and writers, Anderson's sentiment seems curiously old-fashioned. Even a fellow worker in the vineyard of the grotesque, Flannery O'Connor, has expressed her disappointment at the bittersweet taste of his "twisted apples." "I don't really like them," she wrote about the *Winesburg* stories, "but it is hard to say why. Perhaps it is only a matter of temperament. My own use of the grotesque is more flat-footed than Anderson's and my conception of it involves a consciously religious element, which I take it his does not. These stories in W. O. are very humorless. Overcompassionate, maybe."

Still, for better or for worse, Anderson established in modern American literature the use of the grotesque as a metaphor for the inner failure of the contemporary man. Indeed, *Winesburg, Ohio* is startlingly modern in the way in which it gives a sense of the defects of society through the deformity of its citizens. Anderson's vision of the grotesque, possibly the purest in modern fiction, is, like so much contemporary literature, based ultimately not on the deviation from the norm but on the corruption of the perfect, which points up Baudelaire's remark about the grotesque, that "human laughter is intimately linked with the accident of the Ancient Fall, of a debasement both physical and moral." Yet the sweetness that Anderson found in his "twisted apples" was to be drained by succeeding generations of writers who have used the grotesque not as an elegiac symbol of failure but as a satiric symbol of absurdity.

In the work of Nathanael West grotesque satire came into its own. Significantly, West worked in the Holly-wood dream factory and was the brother-in-law of the humorist, S. J. Perelman. Both seem to have influenced West's weakness for slapstick black humor and his fasci-nation with the mythology of popular culture. Thus in successive novels West satirized the spirituality of news-papers, the practicality of the American dream, and the morality of Hollywood. As West put it in *Miss Lonely-hearts*, "Prodded by his conscience, he began to general-ize. Men have always fought their misery with dreams. Although dreams were once powerful, they have been made puerile by the movies, radio and newspapers. Among many betrayals, this one is the worst."

Despite its fantastic qualities, West's work is clearly a product of the thirties. *Miss Lonelyhearts,* his most per-fect evocation of the grotesque, captures the bleak crisis of the Depression in much the same terms as Steinbeck's *In Dubious Battle.* But here West is primarily concerned with the moral implications of a bankrupt society in which "the Susan Chesters, the Beatrice Fairfaxes and the Miss Lonelyhearts are the priests of twentieth-cen-tury America." Miss Lonelyhearts' problem is that he begins to take his role as "priest" literally, to see that the problems his readers present to him are less social than spiritual. Here is one such problem:

Dear Miss Lonelyhearts—

I am sixteen years old now and I don't know what to do and would appreciate it if you could tell me what to do. When I was a little girl it was not so bad because I got used to the kids on the block making fun of me, but now I would like to have boy friends like the other girls and go out on Saturday nites, but no boy will take me because I was born without a nose—although I am a pretty good dancer and have a nice shape and my father buys me pretty clothes.

I sit and look at myself all day and cry. I have a big hole in the middle of my face that scares people even myself so I can't blame the boys for not wanting to take me out. My mother loves me, but she crys terrible when she looks at me.

What did I do to deserve such a terrible bad fate? Even if I did do some bad things I didn't do any before I was a year old and I was born this way. I asked Papa and he says he doesn't know, but that maybe I did something in the other world before I was born or that maybe I was being punished for his sins. I don't believe that because he is a very nice man. Ought I commit suicide?

Sincerely yours,
Desperate

What begins as an absurdly grotesque letter ends as an absurdly tragic one. For like the others who ask for help, "Desperate" poses an insoluble problem that is ultimately theological rather than social. As Miss Lonelyhearts is drawn into the grotesque world of his readers, he begins to take his role as redeemer seriously. "What a kind bitch you are," he tells his girl friend, Betty. "As soon as anyone acts viciously, you say he's sick. Wife-torturers, rapers of small children, according to you they're all sick. I don't need any of your damned aspirin. I've got a Christ complex. Humanity . . . I'm a humanity lover. All the broken bastards." As Miss Lonelyhearts' idealism turns into fanaticism he becomes the victim of West's joke rather than its perpetrator. Ultimately, one is reminded of the scene in West's first novel, *The Dream Life of Balso Snell*, where Balso "came upon a man, naked except for a derby in which thorns were sticking, who was attempting to crucify himself with thumb tacks."

The moral theme and mordant tone of West's best work is echoed in the whole school of contemporary writers known as the "Black Humorists." But nowhere is it better sustained than in the fiction of the late Flannery O'Connor. *Miss Lonelyhearts,* in fact, can be viewed as the model for all her fiction: at the center of her work is the confrontation between the modern secular sensibility and the fundamentalist religious vision. Thus her characters are invariably blind Bettys or fanatical Miss Lonelyhearts: those whose perception has been distorted by what Walter Lippman called "the acids of modernity" or those whose vision has been astigmatized by an older, eccentric but uncompromising orthodoxy. Like West, Miss O'Connor created a wasteland of spiritually displaced persons where, in Yeats' phrase, "The best lack all conviction while the worst/Are full of passionate intensity." In such a world it is appropriate that the alternatives should be stated by a criminal called The Misfit:

Jesus was the only One that ever raised the dead . . . and He shouldn't have done it. He thown everything off balance. If He did what He said, then it's nothing for you to do but thow away everything and follow Him, and if He didn't, then it's nothing for you to do but enjoy the few minutes you got left the best way you can—by killing somebody or burning down his house or doing some other meanness to him.

Though the humor in this passage is appropriately black, Miss O'Connor's vision was distinguished from other dealers in the grotesque by the fact that she was both a Southerner and a Catholic. Consequently, she drew upon the strength of an established cultural scene and an orthodox religious position. There have been many fine Southern writers in recent years and even a few native Catholic novelists of note; but rarely has a respect for region and religion been combined with such impressive results. As Caroline Gordon put it, "In [her] stories, the rural South is, for the first time, viewed by a writer whose orthodoxy matches her talent. The results are revolutionary."

Indeed, Flannery O'Connor's stories exhibit the fanatical single-mindedness of her characters in their concentration on the Southern fundamentalist imagination. While other Southern writers became alienated both geographically and intellectually from their homeland, Miss O'Connor continued to train her sights on the small area of Georgia in which she lived. "Southern culture," she wrote, "has fostered a type of imagination that has been strongly influenced by Christianity of a not too unorthodox kind and by a strong devotion to the Bible, which has kept our minds attached to the concrete and living symbol."

It was this type of imagination which was always at the center of her stories and which made for the remarkable unity of all her work. Whereas the multiplicity of modern fiction is reflected in the varied works of such different writers as John Updike, Wright Morris, and Saul Bellow, almost all of Flannery O'Connor's stories deal with the same settings, situations, and character types. Her vision was deep rather than wide and her development may be viewed as a process of enriching a few themes and plots. For instance, "Judgment Day," the final story in her posthumously published collection, *Everything That Rises Must Converge*, is a reworking of her first published story, "The Geranium." Both tell of an old man's sad transplantation from the fading South he thought he understood to an impersonal New York City with which he cannot cope. But the later story is fuller and richer in every way and, as the title suggests, it adds a religious dimension that became the hallmark of her most distinguished work.

In fact, many of her stories are about old people or children because, as she remarked, "they are both fanatics." In "A View of the Woods," for example, a strong-willed old man and his stubborn young granddaughter destroy each other rather than surrender their respective identities. Similarly, in *The Violent Bear It Away*, young Tarwater struggles against the prophesy of his fanatical great uncle in a desperate attempt to escape his fate. In these tales and others the conflict is not merely between two strong wills but between two generations. Yet both the very old and the very young are alienated from the modern adult world which is rationalized and secularized, bourgeois and dull. Like the old, "children are cursed with believing" and this sets them both apart from the present society of skeptics. As Miss O'Connor put it, "The child and the old person glare at each other from where the two ends of the circle join. One hasn't taken on too many desires and the other has dropped many. There's a kind of comic rivalry between them."

Yet her old men do represent a declining generation with old-fashioned ideas about society and religion. Grotesqueness marks their alienation from the present and Miss O'Connor makes clear the social as well as the moral implications of the passing of the old order. For instance, in "A Late Encounter with the Enemy" an obscure ninety-two-year-old Civil War veteran is exploited by his daughter, his state historical society, and even Hollywood as a symbol of a dying past he cannot even remember. In terms reminiscent of Nathanael West, his dehumanization is described:

Since then, his life had not been very interesting. His feet were completely dead now, his knees worked like old hinges, his kidneys functioned when they would, but his heart persisted doggedly to beat. The past and the future were the same thing to him, one forgotten and the other not remembered; he had no more notion of dying than a cat. Every year on Confederate Memorial Day, he was bundled up and lent to the Capitol City Museum where he was displayed from one to four in a musty room full of old photographs, old uniforms, old artillery, and historic documents. All these were carefully preserved in glass cases so that children would not put their hands on them. He wore his general's uniform from the premiere and sat, with a fixed scowl, inside a small roped area. There was nothing about him to indicate that he was alive except an occasional movement in his milky eyes, but once when a bold child touched his sword, his arm shot forward and slapped the hand off in an instant. In the spring when the old houses were opened for pilgrimages, he was invited to wear his uniform and sit in some conspicuous spot and lend atmosphere to the scene.

The description is reminiscent of Poe's "The Man Who Was Used Up" but the combination of social and moral insight more closely resembles West's *A Cool Million; or, The Dismantling of Lemuel Pitkin*. In both, grotesque distortion is used to reflect the real world in the manner of a crazy mirror in a fun house. As in West, the reflection of the social world is only incidental to the central moral concern. As Miss O'Connor noted, "I am not interested in social customs, in manners, in social problems or anything of that kind except as they might exhibit the souls of my characters. If you know a better word than soul, you are welcome to put it in my mouth."

While other writers might quibble with the word "soul" few, I think, would quarrel with the sentiment. Similarly, Miss O'Connor spoke for many of her contemporaries when she described the dilemma of the modern artist:

My own feeling is that writers who see by the light of their Christian faith will have, in these times, the sharpest eyes for the grotesque, for the perverse, and for the unacceptable. In some cases, these writers may be unconsciously infected with the Manichean spirit of the times and suffer the much discussed disjunction between sensibility and belief, but I think that more often the reason for this attention to the perverse is the difference between their beliefs and the beliefs of their audience. Redemption is meaningless unless there is a cause for it in the actual life we live, and for the last few centuries there has been operating in our culture the secular belief that there is no such cause.

The novelist with Christian concerns will find in modern life distortions which are repugnant to him, and his problem will be to make these appear as distortions to an audience which is used to seeing them as natural; and he may well be forced to take ever more violent means to get his vision across to this hostile audience. When you can assume that your audience holds the same beliefs you do, you can relax a little and use more normal ways of talking about it; when you have to assume that it does not, then you have to make your vision apparent by shock—to the hard of hearing you shout, and for the almost blind you draw large and startling figures.

Though Miss O'Connor may have underestimated the Manichean spirit of the times, she has accurately portrayed the present literary situation. Surely, the concern for the grotesque is not limited to novelists with Christian concerns; neither is the sense of alienation from cultural norms. Thus Miss O'Connor's recurrent images were not radically different from other writers. Like Norman Mailer or John Hawkes, she was primarily concerned with putting her characters into "extreme situations" in the interests of working out their salvation. Just as Truman Capote and Saul Bellow confront their average characters with maniacal *alter egos* in works like *In Cold Blood* and *The Victim*, so Miss O'Connor tests her "good country people" with manifestations of the diabolical and the divine. In "Good Country People," for instance, an itinerant Bible salesman teaches a crippled and cynical girl that she "ain't so smart" by stealing her wooden leg when she had set out to seduce him. "Aren't you just good country people?" she gasps. "Yeah," he answers, "but it ain't held me back none. I'm as good as you any day of the week." In all cases, the protagonist is forced to feel the truth of Kierkegaard's remark, quoted by Carson McCullers in *Clock Without Hands*: "*The greatest danger, that of losing one's own self, may pass off quietly as if it were nothing; every other loss, that of an arm, a leg, five dollars, a wife, etc., is sure to be noticed.*"

In many of her stories this demonic intrusion into ordinary life is the mechanism by which Miss O'Connor's characters achieve a glimpse of salvation. In "A Good Man Is Hard to Find," the old grandmother, confronted by an escaped convict called The Misfit, embraces him as one of her children at the moment when he murders her. It is, as Miss O'Connor suggested, "the moment of Grace," leading The Misfit to remark, "She would have been a good woman if it had been somebody there to shoot her every minute of her life." In "A Circle in the Fire," Mrs. Cope is taught about the limits of private ownership by a band of small, demonic boys. "She don't own them woods," one of them says before they set fire to her property. "Gawd owns them woods and her too." Similarly, in "The Displaced Per-

son" and "Greenleaf" two middle-aged "Christian" ladies learn something elementary about their religion
from violent encounters with a Polish refugee and a slow
moving handyman. Both Mrs. McIntyre and Mrs. May
become victims of their own spiritual incapacity when
confronted by *mana* from such unlikely sources. In fact,
"Greenleaf" contains the same situation employed in
the earlier "Displaced Person" to develop the tragicomic
struggle between the bourgeois ethic and proletarian fun-
damentalism. Mr. Greenleaf is a slow but irresistible
force with a face "shaped like a rough chalice." His
employer, Mrs. May, "was a good Christian woman with
a large respect for religion, though she did not, of course,
believe any of it was true." The conflict between them is
both theological and social:

> "My boys done it," Mr. Greenleaf had murmured, and
> then—"but all boys ain't alike."
> "No indeed!" she had said. "I thank God for that!"
> "I thank God for ever-thang," Mr. Greenleaf had
> drawled.

"Revelation," the most original and powerful story in
the posthumously published collection, explicates this
situation most clearly. In it, Mrs. Turpin, another Mrs.
May, receives a divine "message," delivered by a de-
mented college girl, to the effect that she is "a wart hog.
From hell." As in the other stories, the message comes to
an ordinary person who, like most of us, is keenly aware
of her own goodness and of others' faults. The barb is
aimed not at the obviously grotesque but at the apparently normal, not at the social outcasts but at the faintly
respectable. Characteristically, the final revelation comes
to Mrs. Turpin in a vision before her hog pen.

She saw the streak as a vast swinging bridge extending up-
ward from the earth through a field of living fire. Upon it a
vast horde of souls were rumbling toward heaven. There were
whole companies of white-trash, clean for the first time in
their lives, and bands of black niggers in white robes, and
battalions of freaks and lunatics shouting and clapping and

leaping like frogs. And bringing up the end of the procession was a tribe of people whom she recognized at once as those who, like herself and Claud, had always had a little of everything and the God-given wit to use it right. She leaned forward to observe them closer. They were marching behind the others with great dignity, accountable as they always had been for good order and common sense and respectable behavior. They alone were on key. Yet she could see by their shocked and altered faces that even their virtues were being burned away. She lowered her hands and gripped the rail of the hog pen, her eyes small but fixed on what lay ahead. In a moment the vision faded but she remained where she was, immobile.

The vision is worthy of a Flemish master. In an era of casual apocalyptic utterances it presents us with the real thing. Yet the vision suggests, too, the remark of Thomas Mann which Miss O'Connor was fond of quoting that "the grotesque is the genuine anti-bourgeois style." For the confrontation with the demonic or divine leads to the discovery of the truly deformed: those crippled by bourgeois complacency, the complacency of the morally and materially comfortable. In this context, the perverse and the unacceptable may become the agents of the Lord just as the Misfit becomes an angelic executioner and the demonic little boys, dancing in "A Circle in the Fire," let out "a few wild shrieks of joy as if the prophets were dancing in the fiery furnace, in the circle the angel had cleared for them." For "practical" rather than "theological" people like Mrs. McIntyre in "The Displaced Person," who believe that "Christ was just another D. P.," "the presence of Grace will always be a grotesque manifestation. As Miss O'Connor put it, "Your characters are either going to be guided by the Holy Ghost and their own free will, or be determined by social forces. If what is normal is decided by the society and the society itself is distorted, then those guided by the Holy Ghost are going to be grotesques, as well as those who have latched onto one truth and are riding it to their destruction."

It is this latter conflict between the force of spirit and

the force of society which is at the hub of Miss O'Connor's two novels. But there the field of battle shifts from the ordinary to the extraordinary person confronted by an extreme situation involving his salvation. In a word, both novels are about possessed characters who must accept their religious fate after a long struggle, young men who do not merely catch a glimmer of grace but rather are scourged by redemption. Thus they are less like the middle-aged, middle-class protagonists of Miss O'Connor's stories than like the demonic antagonists of those tales who must murder in order to create. It is as if, by a twist of the lens, the reluctant dark angels like The Misfit should suddenly come into sharp focus. If their histories cannot be compressed into a short story it is because they must not merely glimpse the revelation in a final moment of loss and insight but rather struggle against their destiny to the bitter end. Their lives are not tales of sudden epiphany but of the struggle for revelation.

The situation of the two novels is described in miniature in an early story, "The River." A small boy, who unconsciously assumes the name of the preacher who will baptize him, moves dreamily toward his baptism and his death by drowning. The central scene is a revival meeting down by the riverside in which the boy is the only one to be totally immersed. The preacher tells the crowd:

There ain't but one river and that's the River of Life, made out of Jesus' Blood. That's the river you have to lay your pain in, in the River of Faith, in the River of Life, in the River of Love, in the rich red river of Jesus' Blood, you people! . . . It's a river full of pain itself, pain itself, moving toward the Kingdom of Christ, to be washed away, slow, you people, slow as this here old red water river round my feet.

It is into this river that the boy, Bevel, ultimately immerses himself while the others are content to dip in a hand, splash a foot, or wade only part way in. Thus though Bevel's baptism also leads to his death, the act is significant because, as the preacher said, now he counted.

The heroes of Miss O'Connor's two novels are plunged into the same river of life. While others line the shore they are totally immersed, finding themselves at once baptized and clearly over their heads. Again the heroes are named after preachers, spiritual fathers who force them to take up a burden and accept a fate against their will. In each case, his fate takes the hero to the corrupt city, that hellish place described in Dantesque terms in the remarkable story, "The Artificial Nigger." In the novels, however, there is no Virgil to guide the heroes, only an inner voice or an inner necessity which drives them to meet their fate. It is the scope of this struggle with their fate that makes these novels more substantial than the stories. As Miss O'Connor noted, "Both novels have begun by my writing stories that I saw could be expanded because they had heroes that you couldn't exhaust in a story."

"About Wise Blood," Miss O'Connor recalled. "I was five years writing it and the idea came over that period. I feel my way. It started when I was on a train coming from Chicago. There was a Tennessee boy on it in uniform who was much taken up worrying the porter about how the berths were made up; the porter was so regal he just barely tolerated the boy. I wrote a story suggested by that called The Train." The story, however, lacked the main theme and situation of the novel: bereft of his fundamentalist family and recently recovered from his wounding army experience, Hazel Motes comes to the city from the now deserted village in which he was born. Having lost his home and his religion, Haze seeks to find a new life by cutting the ties with the old and founding a new religion, The Church without Christ. Like a Dostoevskian hero, Haze has come to deny the reality of Christ whose actions he will ultimately imitate. "I AM clean," he insists. "If Jesus existed, I wouldn't be clean."

And like a Dostoevskian hero, Haze meets several characters who are partial reflections of himself. The first is an unattractive adolescent country boy named Enoch Emory whose experiences in the city are a parodic echo of Haze's. It is Enoch's "wise blood" which provides the title of the novel and the proper anti-Christ for Haze's new religion. The second, As a Hawks, is a scarred evangelist turned predatory con man who once attempted to blind himself "to justify his belief that Christ Jesus had redeemed him." Haze tries to uncover the secret of Hawks' pretended blind faith only to discover that the old man's nerve had failed him. In the end Haze must redeem Hawks' lack of faith by blinding himself in the same manner. The third mirror image is a sad dupe named Solace Layfield who is paid to imitate Haze in order to make money for another con man appropriately named Hoover Shoats. This is the image that Haze must destroy before he can begin to redeem himself.

In the course of the novel Haze's belief that "it was not right to believe anything you couldn't see or hold in your hands or test with your teeth" is tried and found inadequate. First he is duped by Asa Hawks' pretended blindness, then he is deceived by Asa's daughter's pretended innocence. Throughout, he mistakes the false for the true and is constantly cheated by city sharpers such as car salesmen, garage mechanics, and landladies. Vision, in fact, becomes a central metaphor in the novel. Like the hero of J. D. Salinger's "The Inverted Forest," Haze cannot adjust his double vision: he dons his mother's glasses in order to read the Bible but the lenses distort the world around him. When Haze finally gives them up he gives up reading but not seeking. Thus Sabbath Lily Hawks, the preacher's daughter, is attracted to him because of the way his eyes can look at something without focusing. She finds it sexy, but we find it symptomatic of his spiritual myopia. Even his professed heretical religion is undercut by his blindness to its implication. When his landlady asks suspiciously what kind of a church he is preacher of, he replies The Church without Christ. When she asks if it is "Protestant . . . or something foreign" he replies politely that it is Protestant.

Wise Blood is about the blind who come to see and the seeing who are blind. Haze's spiritual odyssey reverses his physical: only when he is blind does he begin to see the light. For Asa Hawks, on the other hand, blindness, though a ruse behind which he may hide his unbelief, is an appropriate metaphor for his lack of faith. Like the others in the novel he cannot accept anything he cannot see, touch, or chew. Enoch, too, can only see things literally. Thus when Haze says that his Church without Christ needs a new Jesus "that's all man, without blood to waste, and it needs one that don't look like any other man, so you'll look at him," Enoch's "wise blood" impels him to steal a wizened mummy from the museum to fill that role. Sabbath Lily accepts the mummy literally as the offspring of her "marriage" with Haze but he, wearing his mother's glasses, sees it clearly enough to smash it against a wall, thus beginning the break-up of his unholy family. Only Haze's opportunistic landlady gets a glimpse of the light when she looks into his dead eyes and wonders what it is that he sees in his blindness that she doesn't. "She sat staring with her eyes shut, into his eyes, and felt as if she had finally got to the beginning of something she couldn't begin, and she saw him moving farther away, farther and farther into the darkness until he was the pin point of light."

Haze's odyssey follows the typical route of modern fiction. A seeker after truth, he immerses himself in Experience which first corrupts him and then makes him sadder but wiser. The search for Experience is the quest on which most modern heroes embark but Haze surpasses them in discovering the suggestion of the world of spirit that lies beyond his senses. Enoch Emory's odyssey is a parody of Haze's. While Haze accepts his role as inner-directed Seeker, a true Protestant, Enoch wishes for nothing more than other-directed acceptance: "He wanted to become something. He wanted to better his condition until it was the best. He wanted to be THE young man of the future, like the ones in the insurance ads. He wanted, some day, to see a line of people waiting to shake his hand." Thus while Haze's unconscious model is Ivan Karamazov, Enoch's is Gonga the Gorilla, a Hollywood star whom Enoch meets at a personal appearance. Just as Haze discovers that Hawks is not really blind, so Enoch discovers that Gonga is not really a gorilla. Ultimately, Haze must kill the false apostle, Solace Layfield, in order to replace the false preacher, Hawks, and Enoch must assault the false Gonga in order to become the real one.

Here the antitheses of the novel engage: the presence of matter and spirit, body and soul. Haze, really believing in what he denies—the existence of spirit—becomes what he rejects—an evangelist. Enoch, believing only in matter, becomes what he really desires—an animal. Haze's religious fall and Enoch's Darwinian descent conspire to present the main theme of the novel: the rejection of the divine spirit in favor of the mundanely material must lead to the violent dehumanization of man. In refusing the scheme of redemption, the characters in *Wise Blood* take on the qualities of animals. Either their names betray their bestial nature (Asa Hawks, Hoover Shoats, Gonga the Gorilla) or they stand as ironic comment on their lapse from grace (Sabbath Lily Hawks, Solace Layfield, Onnie Jay Holy). Thus while Asa has the expression of "a grinning mandrill," Enoch has "a fox-shaped face." In this world of corrupted values, a con man's card table becomes an "altar," Haze's "rat-colored" auto becomes a church and Enoch's washstand becomes a "tabernacle."

The microcosm of this predatory world is presented in a tableau that Haze comes upon at a rural gas station. Here he finds a cage bearing a sign: "Two deadly enemies, Have a look free."

There was a black bear about four feet long and very thin, resting on the floor of the cage; his back was spotted with bird lime that had been shot down on him by a small chicken hawk that was sitting on a perch in the upper part of the same apartment. Most of the hawk's tail was gone; the bear had only one eye.

Those adept at reading signs should have no trouble with this grotesque metaphor of the modern world. Without a scheme of sin and redemption we are reduced to a mock Darwinian struggle for survival. Deprived of the vanishing rural world of his childhood, Haze is propelled into the new South whose transformation Miss O'Connor viewed with mixed feelings. "The anguish," she remarked, "that most of us have observed for some time now has been caused not by the fact that the South is alienated from the rest of the country, but by the fact that it is not alienated enough, that everyday we are getting more and more like the rest of the country, that we are being forced out, not only of our many sins but of our few virtues." It is to this brave new world that Hazel Motes comes so ill-equipped. After his descent into urban experience, his crime and self-punishment, Haze comes to realize that he has reached the end of the line. "He had known all along that there was no more country but he didn't know that there was not another city." Like the hero of Miss O'Connor's second novel, Haze has discovered that "From the days of John the Baptist until now, the kingdom of Heaven suffereth violence, and the violent bear it away."

The Violent Bear It Away is also a novel about a young man who attempts to escape from the scheme of redemption. But now the characters have lost the flat, sharply etched quality of a grotesque cartoon. Though still sharp, they are rounder and perhaps even a bit more reasonable. Tarwater, the adolescent protagonist, and Rayber, his rational antagonist, are drawn with a less brilliant line but with more chiaroscuro. "Thematically the two novels are much alike," Miss O'Connor noted, "though it seems to me that everything in the first one has been expanded and brought out in the open in the second."

The novel concerns a fourteen-year-old orphan who lives in the backwoods of Tennessee with his great-uncle. The old man predicts that, after his death, young Tarwater will follow in his footsteps as a prophet and that the boy's first act will be to baptize his nephew's idiot son, Bishop. Thus Tarwater will save Bishop just as the old man had saved him. The boy is faced with a double conflict: his inner struggle with his prophesied fate and his outward struggle for control over Bishop with the child's father, the school teacher Rayber. But Rayber is also confronted by a dual conflict: his attempt to control his irrational feelings for his idiot son and his determination to convert the boy prophet to *his* scheme of redemption, "back to the real world where there's no saviour but yourself." The action moves inexorably to its powerful climax in which Tarwater both drowns and baptizes Bishop thus accepting his role of prophet.

The similarities between Haze and Tarwater are clear. Both accept their evangelical roles unwillingly and both must go to the city to meet their fate. Both commit an ambiguous crime and both must accept an ambiguous punishment. Just as Haze is forced to listen to the dying confession of the man he murders, so Tarwater inadvertently baptizes the child he drowns. Finally, Tarwater sets out on the road, having accepted his role as prophet just as Haze, discovering that there were no more cities, reenacts the role of Christ.

But there are significant differences also. Whereas Haze must deal with several aberrant reflections of himself before he can transcend their limitations, Tarwater is haunted by a demon which ultimately assaults him before he can obliterate it. Then begins his journey of expiation, an odyssey he has only begun when the novel ends. Thus Tarwater's story is presented in a much more positive light than Haze's. While Haze can only hope for crucifixion and expiation, Tarwater moves past atonement toward his salvation. As Miss O'Connor put it, "Haze's grandfather was a dried up preacher who had Jesus in his head like a stinger, whereas Tarwater's great-uncle is in a broader sense a true prophet. Haze was a kind of sub-Christian; Christ was in his blood and he couldn't get rid of him, but even in the end his acceptance of him never got to the surface. Tarwater too resists him, but in the end he is definitely setting out to be a prophet and has consciously accepted the fact of the cross."

If Tarwater is a more positive statement of the "picaresque saint," so Rayber is a more sympathetic treatment of the skeptical materialist. Like Haze, he expresses a belief in only what his senses tell him but, unlike Haze, his rationalism goes beyond nihilism. For him rebirth means not religious baptism but being "born again . . . by your own efforts, back to the real world where there's no saviour but yourself." Yet Rayber is pulled apart by conflicting emotions over his idiot son.

His normal way of looking on Bishop was as an *x* signifying the general hideousness of fate. He did not believe that he himself was formed in the image and likeness of God but that Bishop was he had no doubt. The little boy was part of a simple equation that required no further solution, except at the moments when with little or no warning he would feel himself overwhelmed by a horrifying love. . . . If, without thinking, he lent himself to it, he would feel suddenly a morbid surge of the love that terrified him—powerful enough to throw him to the ground in an act of idiot praise. It was completely irrational and abnormal.

Like Tarwater, Rayber is also descended from true prophets whose kinship he must try to deny. Literally and symbolically they are of the same family. And like Tarwater, "he knew that he was the stuff of which fanatics and madmen are made" though "he had turned his destiny as if with his bare will." Yet he too is assaulted by satanic inner voices which threaten his reason. "Rayber felt afflicted with a peculiar chilling clarity of mind in which he saw himself divided in two—a violent and a rational self."

But Rayber's rationalistic affirmations are finally a denial of his genuine emotional life and consequently a form of spiritual death. Whereas he has turned his deaf ear to the Word (an affliction resulting from his opposition to the old prophet) Tarwater must eventually heed the voice of his great-uncle. Although the novel is concerned with initiation and self-revelation, innocence and experience, Tarwater's problems are not the usual adolescent growing pains. The boy is caught not only between the realms of childhood and maturity but between the poles of belief and disbelief which his great-uncle and Rayber, representatives of the old and new South, embrace. Thus the battle over the soul of the idiot Bishop is a life-and-death struggle between faith and skepticism over the meaning of human existence. Within this framework the very ambiguities of human action are called into question: Tarwater discovers that both baptism and drowning are effected by the same act of immersion while Rayber finds himself unable to cope with a love so violent that it is beyond his reason. As in *Wise Blood* the ultimate question is one of revelation: of those who seek to be their own salvation, only to lose it, and those who struggle against their own redemption, only to embrace it.

Thus it is fitting that the apocalyptic images of fire and water should be employed throughout the novel. Their meaning is made explicit at the beginning:

The old man, who said he was a prophet, had raised the boy to expect the Lord's call himself and to be prepared for the day he would hear it. He had schooled him in the evils that befall prophets; in those that come from the world, which are trifling, and those that come from the Lord and burn the prophet clean; for he himself had been burned clean and burned clean again. He had learned by fire.

Tarwater too must undergo this travail. Having set fire to his great-uncle's farm, he starts out for the city only to mistake the city lights in front of him for the fire behind him. The city does test his mettle and Tarwater can only redeem his faith through the baptism-drowning of Bishop. After the murder, he is unable to assuage his thirst or hunger except by plunging his head into a bucket of water—the sign of his baptismal rebirth. Having been born again, Tarwater must undergo a baptism of fire which purifies his spirit. When he sets out for his great-uncle's farm, he is picked up and raped by a "stranger," the incarnation of the satanic voice he heeded in failing to bury the old man. After he is initiated, Tarwater sets fire to the unholy ground in a ritual of cleansing:

He stood clenching the blackened burnt-out pine bough. Then after a moment he began to move forward again slowly. He knew that he could not turn back now. He knew that his identity forced him on to a final revelation. His scorched eyes no longer looked hollow or as if they were meant only to guide him forward. They looked as if, touched with a coal like the lips of the prophet, they would never be used for ordinary sights again.

Returning to the burnt-out farm which is now his, Tarwater recognizes that "what he looked out upon was the sign of a broken covenant." The apparition of the Devil confronts him for the last time but now his "scorched eyes" see it for what it is. Tarwater burns the bushes around him "until he had made a rising wall of fire between him and the grinning presence." Discovering that an aged Negro had performed the burial he had abandoned, Tarwater, in a gesture of contrition, smears his forehead with dirt from the grave and then turns toward the city to carry out the old man's prophecy.

He felt his hunger no longer as a pain but as a tide. He felt it rising in himself through time and darkness, rising through the centuries, and he knew that it rose in a line of men whose lives were chosen to sustain it, who would wander in the world, strangers from that violent country where the silence is never broken except to shout the truth. He felt it building from the blood of Abel to his own, rising and engulfing him. It seemed in one instant to lift and turn him. He whirled toward the treeline. There, rising and spreading in the night, a red-gold tree of fire ascended as if it would consume the darkness in one tremendous burst of flame. The boy's breath went out to meet it. He knew that this was the fire that had encircled Daniel, that had raised Elijah from the earth, that had spoken to Moses and would in the instant speak to him. He threw himself to the ground and with his face against the dirt of the grave, he heard to command. GO WARN THE CHILDREN OF GOD OF THE TERRIBLE SPEED OF MERCY. The words were as silent as seeds opening one at a time in his blood.

The concluding pages of *The Violent Bear It Away*
point eloquently past the flat, hard limitations of *Wise
Blood* into a wider, deeper, if less perfectly formed, fictive realm. Here we are reminded less of the cartoon
brilliance of Nathanael West than of the mystical revelations of Henry Roth. For if Hazel Motes reminds us of
Miss Lonelyhearts then young Tarwater recalls David
Schearl, the child hero of *Call It Sleep* who aspires to
speak in "God's tongue." Just as Tarwater is haunted by
his great-uncle's fiery prophesy, so David is obsessed with
the image of the prophet Isaiah's purification by fire.

"But just when Isaiah let out this cry—I am unclean—one
of the angels flew to the altar and with tongs drew out a fiery
coal. Understand? With tongs. And with that coal, down he
flew to Isaiah and with that coal touched his lips—Here!"
The rabbi's fingers stabbed the air. "You are clean! And the
instant that coal touched Isaiah's lips, then he heard God's
own voice say, Whom shall I send? Who will go for us? And
Isaiah spoke and—"

Though David's course is deflected at that moment in a
way that Tarwater's is not, both the orthodox Jew and
the fanatical fundamentalist journey toward the same
"pin point of light." Each pursues the possibility of
grace.

After the publication of *The Violent Bear It Away*,
Flannery O'Connor turned again to writing short stories
but she said, "I keep thinking of Tarwater on the way to
the city and what is going to happen to him when he
gets there, how the children of God are going to finish
him off. I think that is the next novel I'll have to write,
but I guess it will take me forever to do it." In the next
few years she turned out several fine stories, including
"Revelation," and an excerpt from an unfinished novel
on a new subject entitled "Why Do the Heathens
Rage?" "I feel more at home writing short stories," she
remarked, "because you can get them over with in a
hurry, and also because I write from a paucity of inspiration and not from a flow of it. . . . However, I don't
have any sense of having done much when I write a story

now. Everybody and his brother can turn one or two out. With a novel, you never know whether it is going [to] work out or whether you are going to be dead before it."

She died on August 3, 1964, at the age of thirty-nine.

The Sudden Hunger
An Essay on the Novels of
Edward Lewis Wallant

CHARLES ALVA HOYT

Some years ago several of the younger members of the English department of a large Midwestern university were engaged in a discussion with a distinguished visiting professor, Mr. Irving Howe. The burden of the talk—it was too one-sided to be a debate—was as I recall it the unredeemed cynicism and despair of the contemporary novel: "no first-rate novel today has a happy ending." I did not believe it then, and it was not true then, as Malamud had certainly published *The Assistant* at that time; but how out-of-date, how totally inadequate that judgment has become today. What David Boroff has called "the chic despair" of those sophisticated times has been buried in a veritable avalanche of commitment, a revulsion into hope and even joy.

One of the foremost among this generation of commitment is Edward Lewis Wallant. He can be considered "minor" only in terms of what he might have done had he lived beyond the age of thirty-six. I shall not be surprised if future critics award him a high place in our literature on the basis of the four novels he did complete; but in the meantime his inclusion in a volume devoted to minor figures is justified by the fact that he is almost unknown to the public.

Wallant's first published novel was *The Human Season*, brought out in 1960 by Harcourt and Brace. They

118

had previously rejected two others, *Tarzan's Cottage*, parts of which are worked into *The Human Season*, and *The Odyssey of a Madman*, a "long, sprawling, amateurish work," according to his editor Dan Wickenden. Material from *The Odyssey* also figures in later works. *The Human Season* tells how a tough plumber named Joe Berman claws his way back to some sort of decent existence after the devastating loss of his wife. Berman, presumably a recast of the Tarzan of the rejected book, who was also a plumber, arrives at a hard-won state of grace, an almost mystic acceptance of the many wrongs committed against him by his life and his God. The book sold just four thousand copies, exhausting the first and only printing, and received the usual meager critical attention, although with one or two brilliant exceptions, notably a review in *Time*. Eventually it won the Harry and Ethel Daroff Memorial Fiction Award for the best novel of the year on a Jewish theme.

Thus a somewhat more attentive audience was assured to Wallant's second published novel, which appeared in 1961 with the title *The Pawnbroker*. That title at least is probably the best-known part of Wallant's work today, as it was retained for the movie, which however did not come out in the author's lifetime. The book itself had a small hard-cover sale, a first and only printing of 5,000 copies; but paperback sales, stimulated by the movie, had gone to 162,638 at last count, making *The Pawnbroker* Wallant's greatest commercial success up to this time. It is an excellent book, another study of a bereaved man, Sol Nazerman the pawnbroker. His struggles to hide his bruises and scars from his fellow men, to keep his privacy inviolate of the claims of his pathetic customers as well as his assistant, Jesus Ortiz, are unavailing; and he like Berman is eventually forced to come to terms with his past. It is not an easy job, as his experience includes among other things the Nazi extermination camps, which are presented in the novel by means of brief flashbacks, short bursts of blinding horror which have for me few equals in the literature of misery.

On the strength of his two books, Wallant was granted a Guggenheim Fellowship in the spring of 1962. He resigned his job as art director at McCann Erickson in New York and set out with his family for Europe, but before going submitted two new manuscripts to Harcourt and Brace, *The Children at the Gate*, and *The Tenants of Moonbloom*. The question of priority is best left to Mr. Wickenden.

As to which of the two posthumously-published novels was written first, the situation is a little complicated, though to all intents and purposes it can be said that *The Tenants of Moonbloom* was the last book Ed wrote. *The Children at the Gate* and *Tenants*, both written within the same twelve months, were submitted to us (again) almost simultaneously early in 1962, because Ed wanted to know our opinion of both of them before he left for Europe. As I recall, he had spent six or eight months writing, then rewriting, then rewriting for a second time *The Children at the Gate*: it came hard to him, and meant more to him than any of his other books. *The Tenants of Moonbloom* came rapidly, with the utmost spontaneity, and what Ed submitted to us was what he called a rough first draft, although it was in fact a second draft. (His custom was to write, first, a detailed outline; this he would develop into a skeletal narrative; the fleshed out narrative based on this was what he considered a first draft.) We felt, rightly or wrongly, that *The Tenants of Moonbloom* was ready for publication pretty much as it stood, but that *Children* still needed more polishing. We also felt that it might be better to publish *Moonbloom* first in any case, because it seemed a greater departure from the earlier books than *Children* did.

I had better say at this time that this quotation, as well as all other material about Wallant's personal and professional life unless otherwise stipulated, has been taken from a release written by Dan Wickenden and prepared by Harcourt, Brace and World for the use of scholars and other interested parties.

The Children at the Gate, that novel that meant so much to its author, is the story of Angelo DeMarco, a flinty nineteen-year-old who affects a contemptuous skepticism in the face of the ordeal of his job, delivering pharmacy orders to the patients at a great New England hospital. We may go so far ahead of ourselves as to note here that Wallant himself held such a job as a teenager in New Haven. Angelo, whatever his relationship to his creator, is like all Wallant's characters forcefully shaken out of his objectivity, in his case as a result of his encounter with Sammy, a weird, infuriating Jewish orderly who seems compounded equally of fool, buffoon, saint, and savior.

Although *Children* is somewhat lighter in tone than its somber predecessors, it is *The Tenants of Moonbloom* that most nearly approaches the truly comic. It too deals with great depths of misery, the common lot of those who inhabit four crumbling tenements given over by his prosperous brother to the care of the timid, tentative Norman Moonbloom. Although he bleeds inwardly at the unhappiness of his charges, Moonbloom patches away at his conscience as well as at his buildings until, carried away on an irresistible surge of commitment, he hurtles into the midst of the tenants' lives and fortunes with cleansing, purifying zeal. The book is a masterpiece, and the definitive answer to the questions embodied in its opposite number of the thirties, Nathanael West's *Miss Lonelyhearts*.

Edward Wallant saw neither of his last two novels in print. He returned from Europe late in 1962, apparently well but strangely tired and run down. Medical examinations gave no answer, but in a few days he was stricken suddenly with what was at first thought to be an acute viral infection. He lapsed into coma and was dead a week later, in December 1962; it was learned that the cause was an aneurism, or congenital weakness in a blood vessel, in this case in the brain. So the current belief that he wrote his last works under sentence of death is totally wrong, despite the striking suggestions which appear in both novels. Evidence which seems unquestionable indicates that he never knew how little time he had.

In an essay for English teachers, called *The Artist's*

Eyesight (Harcourt), Wallant speaks of fiction in terms which are most applicable to his own art. "Normally," he says, "we see others only as they relate to our own immediate needs, and for that, normal vision is often sufficient."

Yet there are times when we have a need we cannot recognize, a sudden hunger to know what lies in the hearts of others. It is then that we turn to the artist, because only he can reveal even the little corners of the things beyond bread alone.

It is this, the sudden hunger to know what lies in the hearts of others, that is at the center of Wallant's fiction; or rather, as the theme characteristically appears in a framework of exhortation, the absolute obligation of all men to acknowledge this hunger, and to satisfy it by communion with their fellows.

This is the battle cry of the romantics; it does not require much reflection to locate it in central position in such important contemporary works as *Franny and Zooey, A New Life, Henderson the Rain King,* and *One Flew over the Cuckoo's Nest.* Zooey calls Franny back from the edge of a self-indulgent breakdown with the charge to play for the Fat Lady; S. Levin, "formerly a drunkard," takes upon himself a crushing load of responsibility, telling his enemy that he is doing so "because I can, you son of a bitch." An unanswerable conclusion. Henderson of course learns to live among lions, and with his wife and children as well; and Kesey's Chief Broom is reclaimed for humanity along with many of his fellow asylum-inmates, at the cost of the novel's other hero, Randall McMurphy. Not a sad ending in the lot; and there are many other works, some of them superior to these, that might have been mentioned.

The quick sketches with which I have introduced Wallant's novels should indicate how deeply involved Wallant was in the affairs of the new romanticism, which combines the moral concern and savage sincerity of a Nathanael West, a Dos Passos, or Hemingway with a new, sometimes mystical acceptance of life, and most of all, an imperative call to action. Miss Lonelyhearts made several abortive moves, the last one ending presumably in an unedifying death; and when Brett said to Jake, "We could have had such a damned good time together," he could only answer her with what Wallant called "that agonizingly wry answer": "Yes, isn't it pretty to think so?"

No one can doubt that the new romantics owe a great deal to the cynical, unhappy masters who preceded them; but in spirit they are surely closer to such people as D. H. Lawrence, who cried, in *Lady Chatterley's Lover,*

Sex is only touch, the closest of all touch. And it's touch we're afraid of. We're only half-conscious, and half-alive. We've got to come alive and aware. Especially the English have got to get into touch with one another, a bit delicate and a bit tender. It's our crying need.

Wallant says it this way: "We all have to hold hands in all this dark." The words are given to that *daemon ex machina*, Sammy, the orderly of *The Children at the Gate*. To take the hand of one's neighbor may be an unsavoury task, and in any case will prove a difficult one, because all of the wisdom of the world is ranged against it. Yet Wallant like other romantics insists that the effort be made; and the clash of that effort against that wisdom—sensibility against sense, if you will—resounds through his fiction.

Wallant sets up these confrontations with great skill. No contemporary novelist was more gifted in the sheer grace of constructing a novel. He had long supposed himself destined to be a painter—he had earned his living as a commercial artist—and he had also a strong tendency toward the drama. Had he lived, he might have turned to the theater. He left behind him one of his detailed outlines, this time for a play, and he had been thinking of converting *The Tenants of Moonbloom* for the stage. Both of these talents undoubtedly helped to make his novels as graphic as they are. In each one there is a careful positioning of the central figure from the beginning in a fixed state symbolic of his life—in each case, an unsatisfactory life. The characters then initiate or take part in certain symbolic acts which eventually result in freeing them for the kind of deep human relationship which their author demands for all men.

The key word is *separation*. In each novel the hero is set apart, sometimes bound; more often fixed in unproductive orbit around a world of chained sufferers. Moonbloom moves delicately over his tenants, miserably confined in rotting tenements. His rounds originate as simple rent-collections, but end as errands of pity and mercy. Similarly, Angelo goes from bed to bed in the hospital, at first as purveyor of drugstore vanities, but afterwards as a participant in human suffering. The two books are by no means as unrelated as his publishers seem to have thought.

The pawnbroker is fixed at a station: from behind his grille he watches the miserable of the earth as they go by in ceaseless flow. It is only with the greatest difficulty that he is able to persuade himself to reenter their current. As for Berman the plumber, death has separated him first from his son and then his wife, so that he resolves to turn his face from both God and man.

The Human Season, Berman's book, is understandably the simplest statement of Wallant's ideas and as such probably the least like the rest of the canon. Berman's bereavement, the source of his alienation, is personal. Inasfar as death must touch everyone, it is universal; but the actual physical cause of the hero's separation is a personal tragedy. No long lines of sufferers compete for his attention, as in the three later novels; those whom he shuts out of his life are again, personal friends, old connections: his daughter, his partner, God. We find him at the beginning of the book sitting alone like a Bellow patriarch bereft, but he has neither Henderson's money nor Herzog's sensibility to support him. He is only a simple laboring man who has built a modest prosperity upon the foundation of his talents and an overwhelming love for his wife, whose death has left him absolutely resourceless.

An important and fascinating secondary symbolic concept in all of Wallant's books is that of cleanliness, which immediately makes an appearance here. Berman remembers his wife's boast: "Oh my Joe may clean toilet waste all day but he comes to me white as snow." Like other more complex Wallant heroes, the plumber is obsessed with filth, the eradication of which may fairly be said to be his life's work. And Berman's rehabilitation proceeds along this symbolic path, marked by a series of brilliant episodes. In the depths of his misery, for example, early in the book (and appropriately, in the lower reaches of a foul cellar), the plumber doggedly pursues his work, impelled by his hatred of the dirt around him.

"Filth," he snarled, and fumbled around him for something to throw. But everything in reach was insubstantial, and in sudden, desperate rage, he pulled the wrench off the pipe and swung it savagely at the upright rat. The splash was muffled by the soft, crushed body. He pushed it away with the head of the wrench and turned back to the pipe. "Filthy shitten crap," he moaned.

Presently he extends his reproaches, in identical terms, to include the Deity:

Oh-h-h-h, oh. Oh, you shit God, you terrible filth. . . . Damn you, damn you.

Probably the low point of the book is that at which he flings himself down, in all the grime of his work, upon his wife's clean bed.

His face was malevolent as he went in all his filth to the bedroom and lay down on the immaculate, soft blanket. His shoes had bits of ash clinging to the soles. He saw the dirt soil the blanket. He felt masked with grease, except for the long lines of naked skin where his tears had run, like rents in the covering of dirt on his face.

But later, when, "absently" flirting with suicide, he slashes his wrists, he desists automatically with the realization that he is spotting the rug. The habits of a lifetime have saved him.

Then he noticed the red splashings on the floor, one spot on the immaculate gray throw rug. He made a little clucking sound behind his teeth.

That little clucking sound has a more pathetic ring in the ear than many a long speech in Renaissance tragedy.

Counter to the forward progress of the action of *The Human Season* is a series of flashbacks, beginning with the night before the wife's death and probing back deep into Berman's childhood in Russia. These are done with great delicacy, each one suited to the forward action it accompanies. Thus the suicide scene, dated July 1956, is followed by another dated September 1910, in which the boy Berman faints in the synagogue during Yom Kippur. Despite a movement to let him off from his obligation, he hearkens to his father: " 'He will not eat until the sunset,' he said in a stern voice. 'Do you understand, my son?' "

"I would not break the Fast, Father," Berman said in a weak voice from the ground.

"No, you would not," the man said gently.

Wallant carefully guides his character back to health. Berman decides to take in boarders, an experiment which doesn't work, except as a sign of renewed effort on his part. He makes an abortive attempt upon the flimsy virtue of his cleaning woman, and finally drifts into slashing his wrists, until eventually his almost perfunctory curses are answered by a bolt from heaven, or some place near it. Having sunk into a gross dependence upon the mechanical and solipsist consolation of TV, he is roused into anger at the failure of the set. He thrashes stupidly about amongst its wiring, only to be thrown flat on his back, "as though by a gigantic hand."

In the emptiness he began to cry, a simple, child-like weeping. Then, because there was nothing else, because his thoughts and his grievances were amputated for the moment, and he was left only with some of the old reflexes of the spirit, he began to moan:

"*Baruch atah Adonoi* . . . God in Heaven . . . Mary, Mary my wife . . . forgive me. . . . *V'yiskadash* . . . *Gott in Himmel* . . . forgive me. . . ."

Although he would not take the rabbi's story of Job, God has answered him too out of the whirlwind. After a voyage out into the world, during which he participates fully in its foolishness, he packs up his past, clears his house, and makes ready to move in with his daughter.

"Go on, Berman," he said . . . "who you fooling? You knew all the time; inside you musta known what was out there in the dark. For a long time you knew it wasn't a God with a beard just out to get you."

His last remarks to himself, as the novel closes, are expressed in terms that can only be called Wordsworthian: "Answers come in little glimmers to your soul, most clearly in childhood."

"It's like a light that don't last long enough to recognize anything. But the light itself, just that you seen it . . . that's got to be enough. . . ." And then more emphatically, almost desperately, for it was his last hope: "It *is* enough!"

And then Joe Berman "sighed for the last time in the dusty, abandoned room."

Wallant's wife's father was a plumber and a widower, and he himself had a Russian-born grandfather who talked about the old country; and "I was the grandchild who listened." He also had a relative who ran a pawnshop in Harlem. According to Wickenden, "Ed spent many hours there, watching people come and go." This experience, added to those of a close friend of his who was a survivor of the Nazi death camps, provided him with the material for *The Pawnbroker*. With this novel Wallant moves closer to the thing he is investigating: Sol Nazerman too is estranged from humanity because of the wrongs he has endured, but his suffering is at least part of a worldwide agony. At this point Wallant has not yet got to the heart of the sin, which is ignoring other people for no reason at all. This Dante knew well, incidentally; he reserves a particularly disagreeable antechamber of Hell for those who took no stand one way or the other, and are thus beneath the notice even of punishment. "Pass them by," Virgil says.

Nazerman lurks behind an "elaborate series of locks," "burglar alarms," and "heavy wire screening"—"This much-maligned calling had brought him the one commodity he still valued—*privacy*." No illusions for him; "no fear that *he* could be taken in." But a later Wallant character learns that illusions are above all necessary to life. Formerly a professor, the pawnbroker drags out his existence with only a few shreds of his scholarship clinging to him. He has dropped into a filthy business, financed by gangsters, whoremasters. Flashbacks of awesome horror prove his title to his place; the first, for example, shows him crushed with his family into the camp-bound cattle car, utterly unable to keep his little son from sliding into the thick carpeting of feces under their feet. Blistering hate rebounds upon himself and his own helplessness, with the redoubled energy of the heartbreaking reproaches of his wife, the cries of his children, all of them not only slaughtered, but unutterably debased in the process. These passages are of such an intensity of misery that the mind loathes itself for recurring to them.

Nazerman has a right, perhaps, to despise humanity; a right to wrap himself in triple steel against its claims. Yet the book opens to find even his armament cracking under the pressure of long-disavowed duty to mankind. For example, he has just learned that the gangster-backer of his pawnshop is connected also with prostitution, and he will even at this date risk the loss of everything rather than continue in such an association. His wife was the victim of enforced prostitution at the camp.

There is injustice in his own house, too, among his

sister's family, which pursues its will to respectability with a relentless heartiness which is almost indecent in the light of the pawnbroker's history. The boy of the family is at the bottom of the pecking order; his life is so wretched that he thinks of killing himself, but Uncle Sol remains aloof, as ever. As his "anniversary" approaches —the date of the murder of his family—he strikes out more desperately than ever against all those who have claims upon him, scattering the wretched slum people who have depended upon his tiny bounty for such crumbs of decency as their lives can afford. Among these is his assistant, Jesus Ortiz, to whom he stands almost in the relationship of a father, or would if he would let it be so. He teaches Ortiz the mysteries of the craft, the five tests for gold, the seven grades of diamonds. But he betrays the boy by telling him to put his trust only in money:

Next to the speed of light, which Einstein tells us is the only absolute in the universe, second only to that I would rank money. There, I have taught you The Pawnbroker's Credo, Ortiz. What else is there to know?

The assistant is not fooled, although he appears to acquiesce, with typical buffoonery:

And yet, underneath the raillery and the cynicism, there was a peculiar anger, a look that inexplicably suggested regret and accusation.

This advice is almost the death of the pawnbroker, since Ortiz is planning to rob the store with several confederates, the details of whose lives, by the way, add an excellent chapter to the large current literature of the Negro. In the meantime Nazerman cannot resist the claim of two women upon his love and support; one of them is a relic of Belsen, the other a plump spinster, an out-of-towner working for a youth center, full of wholesome purpose and charm. As the terrible anniversary arrives, so does the robbery; but Ortiz, seeing his employer threatened by a gun, suddenly rushes forward and receives the bullet himself. He saves Sol's life, and loses his own in the process.

All of the pawnbroker's defenses fall away from him — "everything he thought he had conquered rose up from its sham death and fell upon him."

What was this great, agonizing sensitivity and what was it for? Good God, what was all this? *Love?* Could this be *love?*
.   .   .   .
Oh no, not love! For whom? All these dark, dirty creatures? They turn my stomach, they sicken me. Oh, this din, this pain and thrashing.

He calls upon his nephew: "I need you to help me." The boy will come to him. And then he is able to weep for all his dead at last: "All the dammed up weeping had been released by the loss of one irreplaceable Negro who had been his assistant and who had tried to kill him but who had ended by saving him." And he walks on, enduring, "if not happily, like a martyr, at least willingly, like an heir."

It will be seen at once that there is a strong resemblance between *The Pawnbroker* and Malamud's *The Assistant*. Both novels give us a small businessman bedevilled by an assistant who is at once a curse and a blessing. These assistants begin as threats but end as saviors. Even more important than plot similarities is the theme common to both — the communion of mankind, founded upon suffering. "It's so lonely not to suffer, so *lonely*." That statement however comes not from a Malamud character but from "one Samuel Abel Kahan, lately an employee of Sacred Heart Hospital" — the demonic Sammy of *The Children at the Gate.* This book, Wallant's most difficult, picks up the thread of the investigation where *The Pawnbroker* leaves it, and carries it to new subtleties, new achievements.

Sammy like Frank Alpine performs the function of catalyst. With Malamud it is the Italian Alpine who enters the Jew Bober's life, changing it irrevocably; with Wallant the Jew operates upon the Italian. If Wallant

in his later works reminds us more and more of Malamud, it is probably because he had by the time of their
writing arrived at more of the older writer's awareness of
the complexity and subtlety of the Jewish tradition as a
response to the great fundamental questions, posed in
their harshest modern terms. One senses, not example
and imitation, but the common tradition. Malamud for
his part has been at some pains to extend his findings to
cover the whole of mankind, and in that most important
way he is not to be classified as a "Jewish writer." Wallant too, particularly in *The Children at the Gate*—the
title comes from *Ash Wednesday*—moved strongly in
the same direction.

The hero of the third novel is a nineteen-year-old boy
of Italian extraction, Angelo DeMarco, nominally a
Roman Catholic but in fact a skeptic of the most hard-
ened sort. Like the pawnbroker he is merciless with what
he calls "delusion," but he has less reason to be so. True,
his life is packed with sordid boredom—a hopeful misun-
derstanding mother, a grudging uncle, a mentally
stunted sister who depends on him. He has escaped these
tedious realities into something very much like old-fashioned Godwinian materialism; the work of the novel,
one realizes, will be to pry him out of it.

When others had murmured piously that his father had gone
to heaven, he had punctured the image by learning about the
electric impulses of the brain and the nature of organic
decomposition.

Like his predecessors among the novels he makes a great
point of cleanliness; he considers throwing his mother's
wealth of religious gimcrackery into the rubbish, "not in
malice or anger, but simply in his passion for
neatness."

Into his carefully organized, tightly circumscribed
world there comes a terrible destructive impulse, a force
which, for the first time in his clenched little life, he is
unable to understand or control. He has the job of taking drugstore orders to the patients confined in the huge

hospital of the Sacred Heart. Nothing less than a blind fastidiousness will serve to carry one through these halls untouched, and Angelo has cultivated his with care. For him there will be no religious alibis, which he rejects in characteristic terms: "All around me I see people making fancy filth. Why can't they be clean and honest?" Sammy, however, the new orderly, is neither. He meddles unceasingly with the patients, even to the point of stealing dope from hospital stores to relieve their agonies. His "white, foolish-looking face" is most often found in the children's ward. Then someone tries to rape a child and he is arrested, but later released when the real criminal is taken—another orderly, Lebedov, a crushed old man.

But Sammy is more trouble than ever. He begins a quixotic campaign to procure forgiveness for Lebedov, getting himself soundly beaten on the way, of course. In the meantime he is driving Angelo mad.

"Whatta you wanta do?" he cried. "Make the whole fucken world over?"

"Yeah. Yeah, *boychik*, that's what I had in mind," Sammy said with menacing softness.

In vain Angelo tries to get away. He is no peeping Tom, he says. "Ah but you looked. And for quite a while." You don't have to touch the patients, Angelo protests, you don't have to smell them. "Yes you do." The answer comes pat. In Sammy's room, he finds the walls plastered with pictures of people—just pictures of people. Make yourself at home, Sammy tells him. "There shouldn't be anything but people on this earth." There is no God, Angelo says wildly. Well then, the answer comes, "I guess you would say we were all orphans together."

"Leave me alone, you goddam freak!" In desperation Angelo turns Sammy over to the hospital authorities; but only succeeds in setting off the orderly's last orgy of joy. Sammy in the hands of the officials recalls nothing so much as the episode of the Grand Inquisitor from *The Brothers Karamazov*, not at all coincidentally it would

seem, if one knows of Wallant's judgment of Dostoyevsky from *The Artist's Eyesight*: "the writer I now believe
to be the greatest and the only really endless artist of
all." The argument in *The Children at the Gate* takes
place between atheist Angelo, now trembling at the edge
of real human compassion, and Sister Louise, the representative of the church. Angelo brings forward his new-
found wisdom: "Nothing is anybody's fault." And he is
answered:

What a dreadful thing to believe! Why, if that were true,
life would be terrible. There would be nothing but agony.

Shortly thereafter Sammy falls to his death, his last
words "Love me, O *kinder!*"

The Children at the Gate ends with Angelo's reclama-
tion. He has acquiesced, triumphed in the crucifixion of
Sammy, who literally impaled himself on a wrought-iron
spike, and there has been printed upon his own heart a
stigma—"slow massive bleeding he would never be able
to stop." But "although the world would be the death of
him, it would be the life of him too." The book is not
easy. It transcends the Jewish tradition, almost to the
point of embracing the Christian—or perhaps it only
points out their essential likeness. Stylistically it is enormously rich: Wallant's reworkings give it a positive
glaze, a dazzle of poetry and aphorism. Lebedov the
child-molester captured:

His eyes were an atrocity; they could have belonged to a tiger
who acquires, in the midst of feeding on the flesh of a man
he has just killed, the curse of human understanding.

Angelo before some maimed patient:

He counted out her change, hoping his rather gay manner
was a manifestation of resignation and not of spite or cruelty;
he despised cruelty because it was the face of weakness.

It is gratifying to find all this power turned in the
direction of comedy with Wallant's last book. Very
shortly before his death, he is said to have told his wife
that he had discovered that he could be as serious as he

needed to be through comedy. *The Tenants of Moon-bloom* is the fruit of that discovery.

Mr. Ivor Brown, in the progress of one of his rambles through etymology (*Just Another Word*), has noted that for men the lunar prefix is one of contempt. He cites "moon-blind," "moon-eyed," "moon-faced," "moony," "moonish," and "moon-calf," but awards the palm to the sweet Jonsonian "moonling"—"a dreamy fool." Wallant's Norman Moonbloom is not quite that, but the description is not far wrong. Moonbloom's affliction is the most sophisticated strain of the disease endemic in all Wallant's heroes: withdrawal through sheer inanition. Although by no means a brilliant worldly success, he at least has a brother who is, and is willing to share his wealth, if distastefully. There is no prison camp in his background. In person he inclines to the ridiculous, with his over-size pearl gray fedora which makes him look "like a child imitating a gangster"—something like a latter-day unintimidating Max Beerbohm, one supposes. As to personality, he is as ineffectually thin-skinned as some of the minor figures of J. D. Salinger—the little boy of "Down at the Dinghy," for example, who hid in the cellar because a girl told him that there was a worm in her thermos bottle. In short, he is not at all commanding, but he is none the less well suited to Wallant's purpose for that. Tragedy may be the noblest phenomenon on earth, but comedy is a condescension of the Divine itself, as Isak Dinesen has observed ("Sorrow Acre"). It remains for the humble Moonbloom to provide the last and best showcase for Wallant's theme.

Through the agency of the little rent collector, the author reveals to us the rich fetid world of the tenement, which springs into action for the reader at Moonbloom's appearance like Adam taking life from God's fingertips. Mad varieties of ineptitude and vulgarity flower for us, great coarse blossoms of lust, stupidity, and failure. As he wades through it all Moonbloom tries to keep clean, to keep clear, but finds of course that no man can escape contamination by his fellows. Picking his way through the boiled cabbage, the crusted plumbing, the incredible litter, he is forced into a growing recognition of his own responsibility for all these people. He is like Malamud's Fidelman, the silly saint of "The Last Mohican" who is pursued relentlessly by one Shimon Susskind, a foul sponging immigrant. "Am I responsible for you then, Susskind," he finally calls out, and gets this answer: "Who else?"

The difference is that Wallant has now gone far beyond Malamud in his program of action. Moonbloom not only ceases to resist the elements which seek to humanize him—for example, he loses his virginity in a ludicrous way, and he notes with a strange content the fact that his name is eroding from his office window—but he finally takes up arms in an all-out assault upon the entrenched forces of filth and apathy. With his grumbling ally, Gaylord the Negro janitor, he charges into his tenants' homes and lives to mend them all or die in the attempt.

Wallant's descriptions of these sorties are perhaps the high point of his art. From the very beginning Moonbloom is transformed. Now a man of power, he deals out life with both hands, taking much for himself: "Oh God . . . all this for *me*?" First he scours out the cesspool that has been long inhabited by Karloff, "the world's oldest atheist." The old man does not survive the job long, but there is the inevitability of the changing seasons in his death. The work goes on and on to the tune of "the rasp of plaster knife, the swish of brush, the routing, cutting sounds of Gaylord healing walls and floors by the age-old method of enlarging the wounds— things must get worse before they can get better." It is as though Sammy has returned to his task of remaking the world. But Moonbloom is doing it, still wearing his good pants, vest, and tie: "No disguises; this is all happening to Norman Moonbloom."

He falls heir to "even greater intimacies," he becomes confessor, arbiter, savior of all his charges, who fall over themselves in casting their secrets before him for cleans-

ing. In a glorious moment, he shellacs himself into a
corner and stays all night rather than spoil the job. In
the morning, because his hands are too coated with
shellac to feel anything, he kisses the floor to find that it
is ready. Miracles happen. A poor musician tries to kill
himself, but fails. Moonbloom is caught in the act with
his lady by her father, but the old man takes the discovery with equanimity. A former concentration-camp attendant becomes a Jew. The summit, as Moonbloom
remarks, is near.

That eminence is represented by the apartment of Mr.
Basellecci. For a long time this man has endured the
humiliation of a great tumor in his bathroom wall; it has
threatened his well-being to the point where he blames it
for the general collapse of his health. In fact, he has
cancer, as everyone including himself finally come to
admit; but nothing can stop Moonbloom's attack on the
wall. The book reaches its climax as he and his helpers,
stone-drunk with Basellecci's strega, anisette, and chi-
anti, smash the wall to atoms:

There came a rumbling, a choking, a gurgling. The wall
exploded in a wet vomit of brown thick liquid. Norman was
inundated. His eyes and mouth were clogged with a vile and
odorous viscosity, his clothes soaked. The torrent went on
for about eight seconds, then belched and fell off to a trickle.
No one breathed or moved. The other three just stared at
Norman in horror. He was a reeking, slimy figure gleaming in
the harsh light over the toilet. The world waited for his
outcry.

. . . .

"I'M BORN!" he howled, with unimaginable ecstasy.
"See, Basellecci, I'm born to you. See, see, smell me, see me.
You'll be healed. Everything will be all right!"

"But I'll die?" Basellecci squealed in terrible excitement.

"Yes, yes, you'll die," Norman screamed, laughing.

"In terrible pain?"

"In terrible pain."

"Alone?"

"All alone."

Basellecci began to laugh and cry at the same time. "I'm drunk," he wailed. "I'm so drunk that I'm happy."

Moonbloom ends his book in glorious intimacy with these men, "an intimacy no normal men ever achieve." "We must love and delight in each other and in ourselves!" he cries. Wallant's least likely hero has taken the farthest step forward of them all. He now embraces a new credo, a trinity expounded by Sugarman, the intellectual candy-butcher: Love, Courage and Illusion. He has won them and they are his, forever.

It is not hard to see why some readers have imagined that Wallant himself was in Basellecci's case, looking with wide-open eyes at approaching death. And it would have been an excellent thing to say, that there was a man who could write as he did, knowing what he knew. But in a sense it is better as it really happened; it is more generous still. For there is no taint of personal interest in Wallant's message even to the very last; he wrote as he did, it seems, simply because of a general love for, and a general faith in mankind.

Notes

BERNARD — Charles Brockden Brown

1. *The Power of Blackness* (New York, 1958), p. 21.
2. For example, his editorship of magazines like the *American Register, or General Repository of History, Politics, and Science,* his political pamphlets, and his translation of Volney's *Tableau du climat et du sol des États-Unis.*
3. William Dunlap, *The Life of Charles Brockden Brown* (Philadelphia, 1815), I, 54.
4. *The Rhapsodist,* ed. Harry Warfel (New York, 1943), p. 109.
5. W. H. Prescott, "The Life of Charles Brockden Brown," *The Library of American Biography,* ed. Jared Sparks (New York, 1839), I, 129.
6. *Ibid.,* 134.
7. Ernest Marchand, Introduction to *Ormond* (New York, 1937), p. xxix.
8. "Brockden Brown and the Novel," *Sewanee Review* (October, 1910), pp. 442–43. In fact, however, Brown was admired by such English writers as Keats, both Shelleys, Scott, and Godwin.
9. In this connection, see Kenneth Bernard, "Charles Brockden Brown and the Sublime," *The Personalist,* Vol. 45, No. 2 (Spring, 1964), 235–49.
10. On these two books see Kenneth Bernard, "*Arthur Mervyn*: The Ordeal of Innocence," *Texas Studies in Literature and Language,* VI, No. 4 (Winter, 1965), 441–59, and "*Edgar Huntly*; Charles Brockden Brown's Unsolved Murder," *The Library Chronicle,* XXX, No. 1 (Winter, 1967), 30–53.

11. James Herbert Morse, "The Native Element in American Fiction," *The Century Illustrated Monthly Magazine,* XXVI (May, 1883), 389.

12. "The American Pioneer of the New Psychic Romance," *Current Opinion,* LXIV, No. 4 (April, 1918), 278.

13. For example, Brander Matthews, *An Introduction to American Literature* (New York, 1896), p. 225, and F. V. N. Painter, *Introduction to American Literature* (Boston, 1897), pp. 319–20.

14. George Edward Woodberry, *Literary Memoirs of the Nineteenth Century* (New York, 1921), p. 282. Cf. Charles Angoff, *A Literary History of the American People* (New York, 1931), II, 321, on the novels: "Nearly all of them are tenth-rate 'Caleb Williamses.'"

15. Arthur H. Quinn, *American Fiction, An Historical and Critical Survey* (New York, 1936), p. 39.

FARNSWORTH—*Charles Chesnutt and the Color Line*

1. Charles W. Chesnutt collection, Fisk University Library. I would like to acknowledge a debt of gratitude to Mrs. Jessie Carney Smith and other staff members of the Fisk University Library for their help in making the Chesnutt manuscripts available to me, and to the Graduate School of the University of Missouri–Kansas City for awarding me a research grant to travel to Fisk University.

2. The University of Michigan Press has republished *The Wife of His Youth and Other Stories* (1968) and it is currently planning to republish *The Marrow of Tradition.*

3. See Helen M. Chesnutt, *Charles Waddell Chesnutt* (Chapel Hill, North Carolina, 1952), pp. 96, 98.

4. *Ibid.,* p. 152.

5. *Ibid.,* p. 177.

6. Chesnutt collection, Fisk University Library.

MILLETT—*James Branch Cabell*

1. Cabell's dedication of *Figures of Earth* reads as follows: "To six most gallant champions is dedicated this history of a champion: less to repay than to acknowledge large debts to each of them, collectively at outset, as thereafter seriatim: Sinclair Lewis, Wilson Follett, Louis Untermeyer, H. L. Mencken, Hugh Walpole, Joseph Hergesheimer." To the

Storisende edition of his books, Wilson Follett contributed the introduction to *The Cords of Vanity*, Joseph Hergesheimer to *Domnei*, Hugh Walpole to *Jurgen*, H. L. Mencken to *The Line of Love*, Louis Untermeyer to *Gallantry*, and Burton Rascoe to *Chivalry*.

2. Joe L. Davis, *James Branch Cabell*, (New York, 1962); Arvin R. Wells, *Jesting Mosses*, (Gainesville, Fla., 1962); Nelson Jay Smith, *Jesting Pilate*, (University Microfilms, Ann Arbor, Mich., 1965); Lary H. Gibson, *The Dischanted Garden*, (University Microfilms, Ann Arbor, Mich., 1966); Desmond Tarrant, *James Branch Cabell: the Dream and the Reality*, (Norman, Okla., 1967); Charles F. Gray, *The Theory of Literature of James Branch Cabell*, (Norman, Okla., 1967).

OLSEN – Nathanael West: The Use of Cynicism

1. James F. Light, *Nathanael West: An Interpretive Study* (Evanston, Ill., 1961), p. 185.

2. Stanley Edgar Hyman, *Nathanael West* (Minneapolis, 1962), p. 29.

3. Alan Ross, Introduction to *The Complete Works of Nathanael West* (New York, 1957), p. xvii.

4. *Ibid.*, p. 231.

5. *Ibid.*, p. 233.

6. *Ibid.*, p. 70.

7. *Ibid.*, p. 110.

8. *Ibid.*, p. 68.

9. *Ibid.*, p. 273.

10. *Ibid.*, p. 313.

11. *Ibid.*, pp. 419–20.

12. *Ibid.*, p. 411.

13. *Ibid.*, p. 14.

14. Light, *Nathanael West*, pp. 37–41.

15. Ross, *Works*, p. 37.

16. *Ibid.*, p. 29.

17. *Ibid.*, p. 45.

18. *Ibid.*, p. 36.

19. *Ibid.*, p. 31.